Praise for
The Art of Debt-Free Living

No one asks, "Should we be debt-free?" What many don't ask (but should) is, "How can I become debt-free?" Deb Nayrocker's book is filled with practical, common sense ideas. This isn't a book for everyone. This is a book only for those who seriously want to get out of debt – and stay out of debt.
   —Cecil Murphey, Writer, Co-writer, and Ghostwriter of more than 100 books, including *Gifted Hands*, *Rebel with a Cause*, *90 Minutes in Heaven*, and *Committed but Flawed*

The Art of Debt-Free Living will provide you with the information, resources, and how-tos you need to be financially responsible. Deb Nayrocker has written a book that needs to be on every home bookshelf. She shares timeless principles for becoming fiscally fit as she inspires the reader to make choices that result in contentment.
   —Carol Kent, President, Speak Up Speaker Services, Author, and Speaker

Deb Nayrocker knows whereof she speaks. Her book, *The Art of Debt-Free Living*, is thorough, insightful, practical, and enjoyable. It will be a life-changing blessing to anyone who not only reads it but also puts its principles and pointers into practice.
   —Bob Hostetler, Award-winning Writer, Editor, and Speaker

Well-researched, extremely practical and very do-able. By following Deb Nayrocker's principles, you'll recoup the cost of the book in just the first week.
   —James N. Watkins, Author and Speaker

THE
ART OF
DEBT-FREE
LIVING

THE
ART OF
DEBT-FREE
LIVING

Living Large on Less Than You Earn

Deborah J. Nayrocker

A Division of WINEPRESS PUBLISHING

Table of Contents

Acknowledgments

With sincere gratitude to my husband, Craig,
whose knowledge of finance
I have drawn upon over the years.
Thank you, also, to my daughter, Emily,
who read this manuscript
and made helpful comments.
Additional thanks to Dennis Hensley, Ph.D.,
Cec Murphey, Leonard Goss, and Dan Penwell,
who have encouraged me as a writer.

Introduction

Dear Reader,

If you are looking for ways to prevent money problems and become money savvy, this book is for you! Believe it or not, you *can* take control of your money and increase your cash flow without putting your family or future at risk. It does not matter how old you are or what your income is. Learning to live on your actual income and not your future income is not as hard as you may think.

People who follow the financial principles in this book can expect to succeed in life, and success will be on your *own* terms. By mastering your income, you will be able to follow through with your life-goals and to accomplish them more quickly.

I wish you success as you accept the challenge and take the steps necessary to become more financially secure and more content with the lifestyle you choose!

—Deborah Nayrocker

Chapter One

Good Times or Tough Times?

"Yesterday's luxuries are today's debts."

—E.C. McKenzie

Life today is good. We enjoy so many modern-day and technical conveniences. Personal computers, the Internet, cell phones, and digital cameras have all made life much easier for us. We can send digital pictures of our newborn baby or the Christmas reunion to our friends, or we can do our banking transactions at home over the Internet. We can fly to desired destinations thousands of miles away in just a few hours.

New homes today are twice the size as the ones in which the baby boomers grew up. Now every child can have a bedroom of his or her own. Some new homes come with complete entertainment systems and theaters and three-car garages.

The automobiles we own are not like the ones we may remember as children. Some family cars had no air conditioning—and we all managed to sit in the back seat together on our long trips across the United States. We listened to a few AM radio stations along the way. Now our vehicles have CDs, televisions, and navigational systems to tell us exactly how to get to our destinations. Yes, technological improvements and new inventions save us time and money, adding much convenience to our lives.

However, even though our salaries have increased, the expenses don't seem to be covered as easily as we had thought. Why is it that we have more bills and more debt mounting? Why do we have difficulty meeting those unexpected or surprise bills? Why can't we seem to save enough money for our future goals?

Just another New Year's Resolution Not Kept

Many of us begin the New Year with grand ideas of how we will keep our spending in check. Then we find within a month or two that it seems impossible to do. Why is it that some people go through life with essentially few money worries, while others have endless financial struggles? Their level of income may differ very little. Many times those who are more financially secure may even have smaller incomes than those who struggle to keep up with their bills.

I've encountered people in my everyday interactions who talk continually of their tough times and their limitations. They don't seem to understand that as long as they continue in their *poverty consciousness,* their lives will continue as they are. It is that simple! This book offers a new perspective on what it can mean to live financially content.

Together we will focus on the deeper issues of *why* we make the lifestyle choices we do. We will look at money-smart principles and strategies that work. We will examine the importance of developing a mindset of debt-free living so that we can live out our dreams. We will look at examples of people who have less financial stress in their lives. They're the people who use the moneysaving strategies I write about.

I know that change is a highly personal experience and that most of us go through developmental stages in the process of change. Many times change becomes a journey, not an automatic event. But, by acting on what we know we will learn what works for us on this journey. The fact is that financial freedom *can* be attained—one goal and one strategy at a time!

How Well Do You Handle Your Money?

                                    Yes   No   Sometimes

1. Do you make impulse purchases instead of planning for purchases?

2. Do you pay only the minimum required on your credit card bills?

3. Do you have difficulty keeping track where your money goes?

4. Do you struggle to pay the monthly bills?

5. Are you putting off saving for your long-term goals, such as college or retirement?

If you answered *yes* or *sometimes* to any of these questions, this book will help you resolve these issues. By the end of it, you will master your finances and sail into the safe harbor of financial freedom.

From the time my husband and I were first married, we set financial goals. The goals were small and attainable. As we reached them, we set other small goals, and these goals grew to larger ones. By planning as best we could, we aligned ourselves financially for the present and the uncertain future. It did not matter what our level of income was. What made the difference was our belief that we could attain our goals and our persistence to follow through with them. The good news is that *anyone* can do this, and it's not as hard to do as you may think.

Is There Any Way Out?

Some people live in *survival mode* when it comes to money. They live from paycheck to paycheck, aware they *should* set money aside for their everyday and future needs, yet doing nothing about it. Thus, they get caught up in an unchanging cycle of existence.

Sue, a hairdresser, explained that she'd felt frustrated about keeping up with her bill payments. As a single mother, it wasn't easy paying all the bills on her income. She acknowledged that she wrote her bills too close to the payment due dates. What frustrated her even more was that the bank kept charging her hefty fees when the checks bounced. And because her monthly bill payments were sometimes late, she often had late fees attached to her next bill.

Sue said that at times she did manage to put money into her savings account. But the money wouldn't stay there very long. She would soon dip into the account for her everyday emergencies. Try as she might, she could not get ahead financially.

Bob also struggled to live on his income. He tried to keep up with his monthly bills. He had been out of college for two years and was fortunate enough to get a job soon after graduation. However, he found that his finances were extremely tight. He said his "only" monthly obligations were a car loan, two college loans, two credit card payments, and monthly rent. He admitted that if he didn't have so many loan commitments, things would be easier for him.

The Credit Crunch

Today, more than ever, it is easy to obtain credit. Consequently, many individuals and families get caught up in a continuous cycle of debt. Increasingly, Americans are becoming overextended financially. Every month they find themselves facing a growing mountain of insurmountable debts.

One might find it hard to believe that only two generations ago mortgages were available mainly for GI soldiers returning from World War II. Cars were purchased on a cash basis or with a loan for a year or less. Customers had lines of credit with their local grocer only if they were dependable and trustworthy.

Most couples today look forward to owning their own home. Unfortunately, they get in too deep financially by paying too much or buying a home *before* they can afford it. Many families buy "too much house." That is, the cost is too much compared to their income. The high monthly mortgage payments and other expenses of home upkeep soon become overwhelming. They overspend on a home and begin the cycle of financial entrapment.

Some individuals do not mind having debts. In fact, it is a way of life for them. They have a "Charge it!" mentality. I have found that those who choose to live a life tied to debt miss many of the better opportunities in life. Having debt should not be thought of as a *normal* way of life. It is only within the last forty years that we have seen the amount of government and consumer debt skyrocket in the United States. What kept our economy stable before this was a determination to *not* burden future generations and beliefs about borrowing that were based on biblical principles.[1]

It is difficult to tell where the economy is headed in the twenty-first century. However, it is easy to observe market cycles and how they affect many Americans. We have seen how the debt load of the federal government is in the trillions of dollars and is growing, not shrinking.

When times are good or not good, it is best to have as little debt as possible. When times are better and more money is flowing in, one can set aside *more* money for the future. During hard times, those with little or no debt are always the sole survivors. In order for our families to be financially secure, it is essential to free ourselves of consumer debt.

Financial Irresponsibility

There are those whose spending habits are so out of control that even winning a lottery wouldn't help them.

Overall, we have seen a downward trend in financial responsibility in America. *Why?* Many failed to notice the statistics and identify some of the early warning signs of being overextended financially. Let's look at a few of these right now.

Late Payments

Late payments lead to late charges and bad credit. For those who have late payments on their mortgages, it can lead to foreclosure proceedings and repossession of the home. Not making car payments will lead to having a car repossessed. When people make no payments to the utility company, it is not long before their power is shut off. When they do not pay the phone bill, it is likely that the phone line will be disconnected. The list of the consequences of not paying bills seems endless.

Bad Credit

Easy credit is a subtle trap. When those bills come due and are not paid, what was once a convenience now becomes a nightmare. When one falls behind on making payments, poor money habits show up on a credit report. A poor credit rating makes those who sell on credit reluctant to extend credit to you the next time you ask for it. Some reasons for credit denial include delinquent credit obligations, foreclosure, garnishment of wages, and bankruptcy.

If someone has a consistently good payment history record then mortgage lenders, automobile dealers, and others who offer credit will expect this person to be reliable in the future. The lenders will look forward to doing business with them.

Consolidation Loans

The only temporary solution some people see for paying their bills is to consolidate them and pay them off over a longer time period. Many times this only draws out the problem, however. Those poor money habits and problems remain.

Bankruptcies Filed

Though per capita income has continued to rise, borrowing by families has increased at an even faster rate. The rise in the amount of revolving debt is especially obvious and is mainly that of credit card loans. Although the United States economy was stronger in the mid-1990s, personal bankruptcy rates were also on the increase.[2]

The number of people who filed bankruptcy in the year ending September 30, 2003, was more than two million. This was a 7.8 percent increase since the previous twelve month period.[3] These statistics reflect a significant slide in financial responsibility for Americans today. Note the common denominators of a personal bankruptcy profile below:

Average age: 38

- 44% of filers are couples
- 30% are women filing alone
- 26% are men filing alone
- Slightly better educated than the general population
- Two out of three have lost a job
- Half have experienced a serious health problem
- Fewer than 9% have not suffered a job loss, medical event, or divorce.[4]

These numbers do not include business bankruptcies. In *What the Odds Are*, Les Krantz writes that during a ten year period, typically seven in ten businesses will declare bankruptcy or become insolvent.

For those who begin to think that bankruptcy is the easy way out, think again. There is a downside. According to *Consumer Reports Money Book*, "A bankruptcy is recorded in your credit file for ten years and may affect your ability to obtain credit in the future; even after the ten years, many potential creditors ask whether you have ever filed for bankruptcy."[5] Obviously, potential creditors are not in the business of losing money.

Personal Problems

As financial pressures begin to escalate, life becomes less manageable. This not only affects how we stand financially, but also slowly creeps into our everyday lives. We find that we become more dependent on others to help us. We also take our money headaches out on those closest to us: our family and friends.

Suddenly we begin to notice more family discord. Minor inconveniences turn into arguments and bickering. Our stress level increases along with our debt level. The more indebted we are, the more stress we have. The stress and constant worry of keeping up with bill payments cause physical symptoms, such as constant headaches or backaches. Feelings of hopelessness begin to cloud our perspective.

High Divorce Rate

In the year 2000, there were over twenty-one million divorces in the United States. The stress of having to pay the mounting bills can pull marriages apart. It is an unfortunate fact that money problems account for the majority of divorces in America. Yet many couples enter marriage ignorant about finances. If couples cannot manage the essential area of finances, other areas of their lives can easily get out of balance.

People between the ages of twenty-five to thirty-nine make up sixty percent of all divorces. Over one million children are affected by divorce each year.[6] Financial educator Larry Burkett wrote about how too much debt leads to divorce:

> It is interesting that the increase in the American divorce rate can be tracked on a curve matching the growth of debt in the country. I believe that the increased evidence of divorce is a direct result of too much debt. Nearly 80% of divorced couples between the ages of twenty and thirty state that the financial problems were the primary cause of their divorce.[7]

These statistics make one wonder if couples spend much time talking about or planning their financial future when they are dating.

Becoming Homeless

Those who have lost their homes find they have no choice but to move back with their parents or relatives. We see how families' lives are shattered during times of hardship. Today the shelters for the homeless are taking in more families with no place to live. They also house men who once had it all. They had a home in the suburbs, a good-paying job, and a growing family. But they lost it all and found themselves in a seemingly hopeless situation.

Two Major Forms of Credit

Two main forms of credit cause people to get into more debt than they can handle. They are: credit card debt and home mortgages. Let's look at each for a minute.

- Credit Cards

  Credit cards have evolved from being rare in the 1960s to where millions are in circulation today. According to columnist and finance writer Jean Chatzky, the average household has access to sixteen credit cards. Credit card debt in 2001 reached $8,234 per household. This is almost three times more than a decade earlier.

  For every month that goes by where one only pays the minimum amount required, interest continues building and compounding. Let's look at up-to-date information on this popular form of credit:

  1. *How many people in the United States carry a credit card?*

     - There are about 190 million credit card-carrying Americans.

  2. *What is the average number of credit cards held?*

     - The average cardholder has eight cards.

3. *What is the number of credit cards in the USA?*

   • Approximately 1.3 billion, if you include (department) store and gas credit cards.

4. *What is the most popular credit card?*

   • MasterCard for credit cards and VISA for debit cards.

5. *What is the average credit card debt in the USA?*

   • About $8,000 per household on all credit cards.

6. *What is the current average interest rate?*

   • 14.71%.

7. *How many teens from the age eighteen to twenty-one have credit cards?*

   • About 80%.

8. *What is the percentage of "maxed out" credit cards?*

   • Around 20%.

9. *What is the amount of credit card fraud?*

- Card issuers lose about one billion dollars each year to credit card fraud. Merchants lose even more.

10. *What was the average credit line ten years ago compared to today?*

- In 1992, average credit lines were approximately $1,800; today they average about $3,500.

11. *What percentage of active accounts are paid off monthly?*

- Approximately 40%.

12. *How many credit card holders declared bankruptcy in 2003?*

- Two million cardholders.

13. *What total percentage of the population has some history of credit problems?*

- About 25% of the adult population.[8]

Mortgages

One major purchase that leads to unmanageable debt is the purchase of a home. The cost of housing has continued to go up in most areas of the United States. A friend of mine recently recounted how he built his house for only $14,000 about thirty years ago. Today he would be lucky to buy an average-sized lot for that amount of money.

"An average three-bedroom home in 1960 sold for about $10,000. In 1990 that same home sold for approximately $108,000."[9] The cost of housing has increased as the amount of available credit and the accepted length of credit has grown.

The dollar amount of mortgage debt outstanding has more than quadrupled in the past twenty years. Note the *mortgage debt outstanding* numbers below:

1980	1990	2000
$1,465 billion	$3,808 billion	$6,890 billion

In the year 2000 the median sale price of one-family homes in the United States was $139,000.[10] The cost of housing continues to rise dramatically and take up more of people's income.

One might note that 72 percent of American families have home-secured debt.[11] This is not a comforting thought since many Americans consider their home to be their main investment.

How Much Is *Too Much* Debt?

The Consumer Reports Money Book states, "no matter how you get into debt, you should know the warning signs of being overextended." Do you know what they are?

If you find that you answer *yes* to two or more of these questions, you may be at risk:

Are you constantly behind in paying your bills?

Do you tend to earmark all or most of your paycheck for debt?

Does a significant portion of your monthly income go to pay interest?

Do you routinely have to go to more expensive restaurants and stores because they accept a charge card and you are short of cash?

Do you dread opening your mail for fear of finding bills or past due notices?

Do you frequently receive calls from creditors and/or bill collectors?[12]

According to *AARP, the Magazine*, consumers are becoming too extended financially. Besides loans for mortgages and cars, "Americans now owe $1.7 trillion in credit card debt, a figure nearly equal to the gross domestic product of Mexico and China combined."[13] Imagine what it would be like if Americans had $1.7 trillion in *savings,* instead of credit card debt.

Many times it is not how much we make that is the problem. It is how we use the money we have. When we manage our income well, we get the most out of what we have. Perhaps with a few small lifestyle adjustments, we *can* learn to be content with that. If we live with contentment, we can enjoy life.

It is clear that we cannot indefinitely spend more than we earn. It is bound to affect us —and possibly sooner than later. It is not just the *average* American consumers who are finding that they cannot live with more money going out than is coming in; it is everyone.

Our American government continues to increase its deficit, seemingly oblivious to the fact that eventually this will catch up with all of us. We have already seen some of the signs. Why should we expect our national government leaders to balance the budget if some of them have a record of not balancing their own checkbooks? In 1992, the House Ethics Committee reported a major House scandal. Three hundred and three former and current lawmakers had overdrawn their bank accounts![14] Some of the offenders are still in Congress—and some have moved on to the Senate.

Our government leaders need to take heed to what our great American leaders of the past said about spending. Thomas Jefferson wrote: "To preserve our independence, we must not let our rulers load us with perpetual debt. I place economy among the first and most important of Republican virtues, and public debt as the greatest of the dangers to be feared." Abraham Lincoln likewise warned, "You cannot bring about prosperity by discouraging thrift."[15]

Yet today very few of our government leaders encourage us to be thrifty. To the contrary, we are encouraged to go out and buy things in order to keep the economy growing. We know that the government consumes and rarely invests. Although we hear from Washington, D.C., that the deficit is manageable, we are continually warned otherwise by financial authorities. Among them are Alan Greenspan, Robert E. Rubin, and those from the International Monetary Fund.

We are getting closer to the time when consumer confidence will be at an all-time low. We will no longer be able to depend on the government to help or bail us out. David M. Walker, the U.S. Comptroller General, is responsible for auditing the books of the U.S. government. He warned us about this country's deficit and its future. He stated:

The GAO [General Accounting Office] was unable to express an opinion as to whether the U.S. Government's consolidated financial statements were fairly stated for a sixth consecutive year. And I can assure you that the U.S.

Government will not receive an opinion on its financial state from the GAO until it earns one . . . . In the case of the Social Security and Medicare Trust Funds, the federal government took in taxpayer money, spent it on other items, and replaced it with an IOU. Given this fact, why aren't the amounts attributed to such activities shown as a "liability" of the U.S. Government? At the present time, they are not . . . . [16]

David M. Walker also wrote about possible solutions, stating that these would have to include:

. . . raising taxes to levels far in excess of what the American people have ever supported before . . . cutting total federal spending by unthinkable amounts, or . . . further mortgaging the future of our children and grandchildren to an extent that our economy, our competitive posture, and the quality of life for Americans would be seriously threatened . . . . [17]

Stop Spinning Your Wheels

If your vehicle has ever been stuck in snow or mud, you know how frustrating this can be. When I lived in Brazil, our family jeep would often get stuck in the mud during the rainy season. When my father put his foot on the accelerator, the wheels only spun faster. We would then get out of our jeep and assess the situation. We followed through with what needed to be done to get out of the rut (an effortful push forward by all), then we made progress.

Many people today find themselves in a safe rut. They fail to focus on the cause of the problem, yet often wonder why their lives don't improve. We may find it easy to blame others for our hard times or believe that debt is unavoidable in today's culture. However, the truth is that if we're stuck in this situation we are not content with where we are financially.

Until those in debt survey the hole they are in, they will only continue spinning their wheels and dig the hole deeper. Then, if we do not change what we're doing we will continue to go nowhere. *What's the solution?* It is necessary to step aside for awhile, assess the situation, and draw up a new plan.

In the pages that follow we will develop and follow through with a plan of action for retiring debts and saving money. In doing so, we will begin to have less fear of uncertain economic times. Once we responsibly take care of our financial obligations, we can expect not only to survive, but to thrive.

Now we have examined several ways that people may get overextended financially. In Chapter Two we will look at the obstacles to living a debt-free life and explore the reasons why we sometimes get into the money predicaments we would rather avoid.

Chapter Two

Roadblocks to Becoming Debt-Free

*"The rich rules over the poor, and the borrower becomes
the lender's slave."*

—Proverbs 22:7

I doubt that people make a conscious decision that
they will live a life of indebtedness to others. So, just what
causes people to get caught in the debt cycle? Before we can
attempt to change our spending habits, we need to address
the *real* reasons why we choose to live as we do and the
consequences they produce.

What are the roadblocks that hinder us from a life of
financial freedom? Let's take a look at them now. These
include:

1. Our misconceptions and beliefs
2. Spending more than we earn
3. A lifestyle of consumption
4. Overestimating the importance of wealth
5. Making assumptions

6. Denying the problem
7. Unwillingness to persevere and save
8. Ignorance in planning
9. Gambling
10. Blaming others
11. No true desire to become free of debt

Our Misconceptions and Beliefs

Our misconceptions about life and money affect how we live and use our money. Some beliefs individuals have are:

- "Showing high social status is important to me."
- "I can always get money from my parents."
- "When I get a raise, then I can afford to buy a new car (or home)."
- "I'm too busy to take the time to plan a budget or look at my finances."
- "Eat, drink, and be merry, for tomorrow we die!"
- "More money will make me happy."
- "I thrive on having a high debt level, because it forces me to work harder and make more money."

By contrast, beliefs that some individuals may have are:

- "Money isn't the end goal; it's a resource used to attain other goals."
- "How I handle my money today says a lot about what my finances will be like tomorrow."
- "I can only spend a dollar once."
- "Money doesn't grow on trees."
- "Borrow sparingly."

The point is that our attitudes about life and our possessions play an important role in how we live and how we handle our money. If we are fearful that we may lose what we have, we will live accordingly. If we are greedy, our actions will reflect that. Many times greed will cause us to make irrational purchases and investments. On the other hand, when we live with an *attitude of gratitude,* we do not regret what we do not have.

What we believe affects how we live. Some people can easily come up with reasons why they can't follow through with a goal. If they hold to their limitations or what they *think* are limitations, they probably won't get very far. However, those who have an open mind as to what *is* possible are usually the ones who attain their goals. There is no question that when we control our thinking about a goal, we can control our results.

Spending More than We Earn

Do you know anyone who got into serious financial trouble because they *didn't* borrow money? I don't. Clearly, since so many of us carry debt, many of us spend more than our resources allow. In fact, 95 percent of us spend as much as we earn and even more than we earn.[1]

There was a time not too long ago in America when we did not have a system of credit. We paid cash. If we could not afford to buy something right away, we saved until we could make that purchase. We bought only what we could afford.

Many of us are in debt because we are using credit cards to make up the difference for our desired standard of living. When we begin to lower our standard of living we will see an increase in cash flow and we'll be able to have a debt-free lifestyle.

My father told me about a time years ago when his friend was sent to jail for writing a bad check. His friend was not the kind of person to do this intentionally. Still, he was kept in jail until the amount owed was paid, and he was disgraced in their town. Times have certainly changed.

Remember this simple principle: "If you don't overspend, you won't get in debt." When we borrow money, we should have a *guaranteed* way to pay it back.

A Lifestyle of Consumption

Many people have developed a sense of entitlement, to their financial detriment. Wherever we look we are beckoned to buy the latest automobile, the newest style of clothing, a bigger and better television set, and a bigger home. We have heard all the reasons why we should buy, such as: "You deserve it, you are worth it, others have it, and you can't live without it."

Today it is not difficult to find a way to purchase what we want *now*. We are enticed to use other people's money to buy things we cannot afford. The advertising industry capitalizes on our desire for bigger, better, and nicer things. Department stores, furniture stores, and auto dealers are happy to have our business. They may offer what we want for *no money down* or no interest for six months. We can purchase what we want with the department store's credit card and be its preferred customers. We must be careful to check our motives when we do make purchases.

We can so easily dig ourselves into the hole of excessive credit. Mortgage brokers do not hesitate to tell us that we can be approved for the house we feel we need. They often don't tell us just how tight it will make our budget.

Having lived in Brazil and visited other countries, I have observed how people can live with much less than they think they can. With less wealth to work with, the ingenuity of people there abounds with whatever is available to them.

Many of us, however, have more than adequate shelter, food, and clothes. We have so much stuff that oftentimes the stuff controls *us*. We have become the ultimate consumers, but along with more stuff comes a higher standard of living.

There is a correlation between contentment and debt. It goes something like this:

Less contentment in life leads to more debt.
More contentment in life leads to less debt.

Often when we are not satisfied with our present situation we reach out and take what we want, hoping to satisfy our present desires. Even if it means putting our purchases (large or small) on credit, we'll do it.

Overestimating the Importance of Wealth

Many of us subconsciously believe that money and *things* will make us happy, bring us friends, and ease all of our problems. In the book *Balancing the Tightrope*, Perry Powell writes about a survey in which 200,000 college freshmen participated. When asked what they thought was a very important goal of life, seventy-six percent listed *financial prosperity* as essential, but only thirty-nine percent said a meaningful life philosophy was essential.

I once read of an investment advisor who gave workshops on investing and was quite knowledgeable about the subject. A financial planning workshop participant asked him if he personally invested money in the funds he recommended. He responded, "I would like to, but all my money is tied up in my mortgage and car payments." How tragic that this investment advisor had no investments of his own!

Some people think that if they just had the right house they would be happy. So, they take on large mortgage payments, enabling them to live in their dream house. They believe this is the answer to a better lifestyle, but soon find out that their dream house has turned into a financial nightmare for them.

Some folks believe that in order to become successful or to get more business, they need to *look the part* of being wealthy. Their ability to pay the bills each month tells a different story, for looks can be deceiving. Although many American families appear to be wealthy, they are only paydays away from economic collapse. They have saved little or nothing for their future or their children's futures. The desire to have more—or look like you do—is a major cause of increasing debt.

Making Assumptions

People develop money troubles by assuming things will turn out OK eventually. Not only are working adults enticed with weekly credit card applications, so are college students. Students are inundated with credit card applications and invitations to "take advantage of this special offer and make an impression!"

College students today find they are not only graduating with thousands of dollars in school loan debt, but also with huge and growing credit card bills. It is easy for them to put the "extras" on their MasterCard, Visa, or Discover Card.

Morgan was a college sophomore who thought it would be nice to have extra spending money for eating out and other things. She was told that having a credit card was a good way to establish credit. So she applied for a card and soon began charging for purchases such as shampoo, clothes, and gifts. Before long Morgan's spending was out of control. By her senior year, she had put thousands of dollars on her credit cards and had difficulty meeting even the minimum payments.

Many college students assume that when they get a summer job they will be able to pay down their credit card bills. They soon realize the card payments are not so easy to make. According to a recent report, ". . . the average college graduate leaves school with about $3,400 of credit card debt."[2] The cycle of debt begins.

Many young couples also tend to make assumptions about money. Couples are able to get a mortgage based on both of their incomes. They both plan to work in order to pay the bills. But when a baby unexpectedly comes, their plans are quickly altered. Their ability to make the payments on just one income is greatly hampered. Or there may be a job loss. Many of us do not anticipate hard times and yet they are a fairly common occurrence.

We should realize that we are no longer in the Industrial Age but have entered the Information Age. Today's economy is becoming more unpredictable. We cannot assume that the job we have today will always be there for us. Those who were accustomed to having a regular paycheck coming in year after year are now finding that times have changed.

Those in the Industrial Age could plan on being employed by the same employer for years. Today one is fortunate to work for a company with complete loyalty to its employees. Rather, they're primarily concerned with surviving themselves! Many employees are finding that they are on their own if they want to survive.

The numbers of mergers and acquisitions, layoffs, down-sizings, factory and business closings are steadily increasing. Many jobs are *outsourced,* or sent overseas, where labor costs are much lower. An article in *USA Today* reports that United States companies continue moving manufacturing jobs and other operations out of the country. By the year 2015, the United States will have lost 3.3 million jobs by relocation, according to Forrester Research.[3]

We have read in the newspaper and seen on the news the stories of families who once lived in upscale neighborhoods, but were then forced to move out because the main wage-earner lost his or her high-paying job. The children were sad, some even crying, because they did not want to leave their homes and friends.

The families concerned found they had no choice in the matter, however. They never anticipated this would happen, yet they could no longer afford the large mortgage payments and continue in the lifestyle they had become accustomed to. Some may have gotten into the debt cycle because they assumed they would be able to get a new job within months. They put everyday purchases on their credit cards to hold them over, but the job situation did not improve. A downturn in the economy played havoc with their plans.

Some people borrow money so they can invest in a deal that is "too good to pass up." It is assumed that there will be a lot of money to be made. When the deal or investment goes sour, the borrower is left with unpaid loans and huge losses.

Others may think that since they are healthy now, they will always be healthy. So, they do not get health insurance coverage. Without proper health coverage, medical expenses can quickly take a toll on any family's budget.

Denying the Problem

There will be those who simply deny they have a problem with the way they handle their money. They may be procrastinators and prefer to push aside the real issues that cause money problems. They may leave their bills in a drawer unopened, planning to get to them later. But the bills continue to accumulate. The due dates come and go, and then the late notices come and do not go away.

They may resist any counsel or helpful solutions, or they may be the *ultimate optimists,* hoping that someday, somehow, things will work out for them.

I liken these people to ostriches. They hide their heads in the sand and hope everything will work out. They put off what will need to be done sooner or later: face financial realities. When one puts off the willingness to face reality, then it becomes even harder to make things right.

Unwillingness to Persevere and Save

Many of us find it difficult to save for what we want. I find it interesting how easily we set limits on how much our children are allowed to spend. We hand them a twenty dollar bill and tell them that is their limit. Yet many of us will not hesitate to spend ten times as much on an item and put that on a credit card.

Many of us want *now* what it took our parents years to accumulate. We have become accustomed to instant gratification. Waiting until one has the cash for a purchase, or until we are better able to afford what we want, is becoming rarer than it used to be. We don't seem to hear much about persistence and perseverance anymore. Our impatience takes over, causing even more money problems.

Many couples starting out want a home with the latest in home furnishings. Some couples accumulate too much too quickly, not paying cash as they are able to, in order to obtain their furnishings. They soon find their debts keeping them from more important priorities.

Don and Kendall found themselves in this situation. They had a mutual interest in being overseas missionaries. In fact, their dream to be missionaries had drawn them together. However, they did not prioritize what was truly important to them in their lives. They focused on their present wants rather than focusing on their long-term goals.

Early in their marriage Don and Kendall began accumulating thousands of dollars of debt for their home furnishings and other items. Before long, they had children. Then they realized that their debt load held them back from fulfilling their dream of becoming missionaries. Do you know of anyone who did not follow through with a dream or career interest because of his or her anchor to credit obligations?

Ignorance in Planning

Many of us are able to easily tell others the latest price of gas in town, but we aren't even aware of what our current checking or credit card balances are. We first lose awareness of our money, then *control* of our money.

Many couples today begin their marriages not knowing how to manage or save money. Their lack of knowledge in handling money leads to poor decisions and money problems from the start. This is also true of single young people just starting out on their own.

Until we know exactly what our financial situation is, it is difficult to put our house in order. When we take the time to observe the inflow and outgo of our dollars, however, it is much easier to develop a positive plan of action. Putting off the task will not help the situation; it will only make matters worse. When there is no financial plan or budget, financial difficulties eventually overtake us. Thorough financial planning is a key to staying in control of money.

Gambling

Some turn to gambling, hoping they will get lucky and their money problems will be solved. In his book *What the Odds Are*, Les Krantz writes that, "America has been bitten by the gambling bug. On an almost monthly basis, gambling is being legalized at places as diverse as Midwest riverboats and remote Indian reservations on the Great Plains." The eight venues of gambling listed in his book are: lotteries, casinos, pari-mutuel betting, charitable games, bingo, card rooms, Indian reservations, and sport bookmaking.[4] But, what at first seems to be a harmless game turns into a harmful habit that leads to substantial financial loss.

Blaming Others

There are those who blame others for the poor financial situation they are in. They feel helpless and powerless over "forces unknown" that mysteriously cause them financial loss. Some may even believe they have no choice in the matter, that they are victims of their situations.

Blaming others usually gets us nowhere, however. Life is easier if we are willing to learn from our experiences rather than blame others for our actions or failures.

No True Desire to Become Free of Debt

There was a time when borrowing was much more risky for a family. Men and women were sentenced to debtors' prison for not paying the agreed-upon sums of money. Families were separated for years. Delinquent debts were considered a crime much more then than they are today. However, just because the laws have become less harsh today shouldn't make delinquency more acceptable.

Many people have come to rely on the expansion of credit to keep them afloat. This road only leads to a dead end. Unfortunately, our government has led the way in telling us that credit is good for the economy, encouraging us to spend, spend, spend.

There are those who are not bothered by their deficits. Some people are never debt-free because they do not truly desire to be. It can be a lot of fun spending money on credit. These folks have what is called *debt dependence.*

However, the fun can quickly come to an end. The minimum payments on debts alone can take a third of one's total income.

Types of Debt

A family's net worth might look good on paper. However, how much of that is owned free and clear and unattached to liabilities?

Credit Cards

Today it is simple to apply for a credit card. Banks send out millions of credit card applications in the mail. Telemarketers call us about their new cards and list all the benefits. It also becomes easy to borrow the maximum amount allowed on the credit card. When the limit is reached for one card, another card is waiting to be used.

Studies have shown that using credit cards will increase spending by 33–34 percent. This happens to be true even if those participating typically pay off their credit card balance at the end of the month.[5] When we pay with cash, we seem to be more aware of our money leaving our pocketbook.

For those who choose not to pay their credit card balance at the end of the month, an additional average of 15 percent interest is charged on the total amount. When you get a cash advance, there is an even higher interest assessed, and there may be extra fees.

When you make a purchase on credit that you cannot afford, you simply delay the decision as to how you will pay it back. The delay factor snowballs and makes the money situation more difficult later.

Also, when you depend too much on credit, your debt increases and makes you a riskier debtor, which raises the cost of your credit. It is not a winning situation.

Helpful Credit Card Tips

Using a credit card at times is not a problem. However, it could easily lead to a series of problems. If you do use credit cards, follow these guidelines:

- Use your credit cards for items that are budgeted for that month.
- It is best not to put consumables such as food, clothing, repairs, or vacations on credit.
- Pay the balance of your credit cards every month.
- When you find that you are unable to pay the balance for your credit card bills, consider getting rid of your credit cards.

- If you like the convenience of a credit card, switch from a credit card to a debit card. The advantage is that the amount is automatically deducted from your checking account, and it is paid for. The purchase will not come back to haunt you later. Just make sure you have enough in your checking account to cover it and regularly enter the purchases into your checkbook.

The Credit Report

Your credit information is compiled by credit bureaus. It is sold to anyone who has a legitimate interest in providing you with credit, such as a credit card company or bank.

The credit report includes:

1. A list of institutions you have borrowed from and the amount of money you borrowed.
2. Whether you've ever missed a payment or had late payments.
3. Any credit liens (a creditor's claim against your property).
4. Any bankruptcy filings.
5. Whether you have been successfully sued.

When you apply for a loan, the lending institution checks your credit rating and your previous payment history. For example, concerning your mortgage payments, your credit report might state: "One time thirty days late."

If you have a negative item in your report that can be explained, write your reasonable explanation in one hundred words or less and send copies to the three major credit bureaus. Also, send the lender who gave out the information a copy of the letter. An example might be a late payment due to a hospital stay or stolen mail.

Negative items such as bankruptcy will stay on your credit report for ten years. Don't expect that to change. You can get a copy of your credit report by contacting the three major credit bureaus:

- **Trans Union**
  P.O. Box 2000
  Chester, PA 19022
  800-888-4213
  www.transunion.com

- **Equifax Information Services**
  P.O. Box 740256
  Atlanta, GA 30374
  800-997-2493
  www.equifax.com

- **Experian**
  P.O. Box 949
  Allen, TX 75013
  888-397-3742
  www.experian.com

Improving Your Score

There are ways to improve your credit score. You can:

1. Stay below your credit limits.
2. Pay your bills on time and every time.
3. Don't apply for credit as often.
4. Cancel the cards that you do not use.

Consumer Debt

Consumer debt is debt that is used to finance furniture, vacations, cars, and other depreciating and consumptive items. It is similar to credit card debt except that applying for it can take longer.

Helpful Tips on Using Credit

We are bombarded with mass media advertising about what we should have and what we need. One of the most common mistakes people make financially is buying and selling automobiles frequently. Buying or selling a car every year or every other year can be quite costly. Buying a used car can save thousands of dollars and the longer we keep the car we already own, the more money we'll save.

For most families, having a good used car offers the best value in transportation. Drive a car until it is paid off and save for the next one. Also remember that you save more on auto insurance when driving a used car.

When it comes to buying furniture on an installment plan, many times the furniture wears out before the loan is paid off. If you find you need to sell the furniture when times get hard, it is difficult to get back anything close to what you paid for it.

You can find great bargains at used furniture stores, garage sales, or through newspaper ads. It is important, however, to look for quality products since they will last longer and save you the expense of replacing them soon after their purchase.

Getting away from money problems does not make them go away. Some families turn to vacations to get away from their financial or work problems. But most likely the vacation is not something they saved for and the expenses are put on credit. This just delays having to face even larger bills later.

A family may consider a *bill consolidation loan* to combine several debts into one large loan. This reduces the monthly outgo and spreads the payments over a longer time period. However, a consolidation loan is only a temporary band aid. It helps the symptoms, not the problem of uncontrolled finances. It is likely that within a few months family members will be back to their old spending habits. The solution is to *cut off the flow of credit* and lower the runaway monthly outgo in order to pay off the deficits.

Mortgage Debt

More Americans own their homes today than ever before. We have come to expect to own our homes. Mortgage lenders have made it a relatively simple process. However, there must be a guaranteed way of repayment.

Bob Russell wrote the following:

> Young couples often fail to anticipate famines and therefore make serious financial mistakes in their first two years of marriage—mistakes that will handicap them for years. The most common is purchasing a house based on two incomes. Rather than starting out with a smaller house and moving up as their income grows, they estimate their ability to pay on the assumption that they will always have both incomes. So they overextend themselves. When unexpected bills or babies come along, they find themselves unable to keep up the payments and begin spiraling into debt.[6]

Not only is the financial burden a factor when taking out a mortgage, but the psychological burden is more intense than people imagine.

Business and Investment Debt

How many times have we heard about a deal that we could not pass up? Many people have gone for a "great deal" that, in the end, turned out to be a very bad and disappointing one. Be cautious and make sure the numbers and facts add up before you invest in something. Is the opportunity presented with a sense of urgency? Do not rush into it. Talk it over with your husband or wife for agreement and confirmation. Discuss the idea with knowledgeable second or third parties. The bottom line is this: Is the rate of return more than the cost after taxes?

Remove the Roadblocks

We have seen how we can get ourselves into a position of financial hardship. Now we must consider some of the roadblocks in our path we need and begin removing them.

First, we should identify our spending patterns. What emotional needs, such as insecurity, loneliness, or deprivation, cause us to overspend month after month? We may find that we continually purchase items that are not absolutely necessary to fill emotional "holes."

Are we preparing for tougher economic times down the road? They will come, and it *is* possible to free ourselves of obligations and not be burdened by them any longer. We can change our thinking and, consequently, our reality.

Remember: our pre-conditioned thoughts determine the logic we go by. Many of us have been conditioned to believe that debt is and always will be a way of life for us.

We believe that it is unavoidable. Maybe we believe we will never be able to get ahead. But that's not true!

In order for us to develop a debt-free mindset our old ways of thinking need to be altered. As we change our way of thinking, then acting, we will notice the added benefits of more patience and greater endurance.

In Proverbs 23:7, King Solomon said, "For as a man thinks in his heart, so is he." [7] If we continually think and say we cannot control our lives or the results of our choices, we will reap what we sow. As we study the patterns in our own lives that limit us, we can look for ways to improve and change them and, with diligence, make positive and lasting changes.

Chapter Three

The Benefits of Debt-Free Living

"An authentic person does not make impulsive decisions."
—Neil Clark Warren

List Your Life Goals

Think about what is important to you in your life. Reflect on what you would like to accomplish or what you would like your family to accomplish. Have you been able to do the things that truly matter to you? Your values will be reflected in your goals.

Take time now to list your goals. (Use the *My Life Goals Worksheet* at the end of this book). Write down what you would like to achieve, from personal to financial goals. Begin each goal statement with a strong verb, such as *complete*, *earn*, *choose*, or *give*. Examples of goals might be:

A. Lifestyle Goals:

- Join a gym and go three times a week.

- Move out of our apartment and into a new home.
- Replace my car.

B. Education Goals for Self or Children:

- Attend at least two seminars a year on investing.
- Complete my Bachelor of Arts degree in four years.
- Pay at least half of our children's college tuition.

C. Family Goals:

- Visit my ailing parents at least once a week.
- Eat our evening meals together as a family.
- Set aside time to help my children with their homework.

D. Career Goals:

- Subscribe to a magazine specializing in my area of interest—and read it.
- Save ten percent of my income for a part-time business.
- Begin a part-time business within two years.

E. Vacation Goals:

- Cut airfare costs by purchasing discount fares at least three weeks before our vacations.

- Plan a trip to Hawaii.
- Learn conversational Italian before visiting Italy.

F. Savings Goals:

- Save $8,000 for the purchase of a used car.
- Set aside $500 every month for our children's private school expenses.
- Open five savings accounts at the credit union, identifying a purpose for each one.

G. Investment Goals:

- Open a money market mutual fund.
- Research twenty stock funds and invest in at least one.
- Open a Roth IRA account.

H. Insurance Goals:

- Investigate ways we can curb costs on our car insurance payments.
- Buy life insurance.
- Increase the deductible on our health insurance.

I. Giving Goals:

- Increase my giving to ten percent of my income.
- Cut down on nonessential purchases to increase my giving.

- Write my giving checks on or around my paydays.

Prioritize Your Goals

Now that you have made a list of your goals, go back and look at each of the goal areas. Prioritize your goals, numbering them accordingly. For example, when it comes to insurance, your first priority may be to buy life insurance. Secondly, you want to increase the deductible on your health insurance so you will have smaller monthly payments. Last of all, you will investigate ways to lower your car insurance payments.

Financial Benefits

We will examine the advantages of having no debt and how our lives can be more fulfilled by having our earning power equal our *yearning power.* When not confined by our financial burdens, we gain enormous financial, psychological, and physiological benefits. Below are just a few.

Surplus Money

Paying off our debts allows us to have surplus money, increasing cash flow. This enables us to no longer focus on our bills, but on other things in life besides ourselves and our money problems. We can then redirect our income and time to our long-term goals and dreams.

Full Ownership

If we borrow someone else's money, even though we may be current on all our monthly payments, we are still under the lender's authority. For example, when we become delinquent on car loan payments, we can expect to have our car repossessed. However, we will not lose our assets when our obligations are paid in full. We are the rightful owners and we retain full ownership.

A More Stable Financial Position

You have probably heard the Golden Rule: "Do unto others as you would have them do unto you." However, there is another *Golden Rule* that states: "Those with the gold make the rules." Think for a moment how true that is!

For example, when we take a vacation, it is generally the person who is paying who makes the final decisions. That person decides where we will lodge and where we will eat. Those who have the "gold" are more *independent*. Those who don't have the "gold" are more *dependent*. Without a doubt it is more satisfying to be the one *with* the gold.

We cannot plan for what will happen in our economy from year to year. But we can do our best to prepare for an uncertain future.

Be More Prepared for a Job Loss

In today's rapidly cycling business environment, we can no longer expect long-term security in our jobs. However, when we have our credit obligations taken care of, the loss of a job is less devastating. We can then depend on the emergency and savings funds we have set aside to get us through the hard times.

Author Bob Russell wrote that, "more than twenty-five percent of the average family's income goes to debt retirement, not including their home mortgages. Four out of five of us owe more than we own."[1] Growing families have a way of outgrowing everything—especially their incomes.

Living More on Less

When we have fewer financial obligations, we are able to live on less income. When we use our own cash money for purchases, we can completely eliminate interest payments, saving thousands of dollars over time.

I have often heard people comment that they just don't know *why* they can't get ahead. A likely reason may be that much of their income is already spoken for.

Positive Interest Compounding

It is much more fun to *earn* interest than to *pay* interest. When we have savings funds that are compounding interest working for us, we are on our way to meeting our long-term goals. Our monthly earnings keep growing, generating positive income. The magic of compound interest helps us to handle financial emergencies and to attain our financial goals. Albert Einstein said that compound interest was the greatest discovery he had seen in his lifetime.

The "Rule of 72" helps you calculate the time value of money. When you divide 72 by the return rate, you get the number of years it will take to double your money. When you divide 72 by the number of years you plan to invest your money, you get the return rate needed to double the sum in that number of years. Note the following examples:

- If the interest rate is four percent, your money will double in 18 years
(72 divided by 4 =18).

- If the interest rate is eight percent, your money will double in 9 years
(72 divided by 8 = 9).

- If you want to double your money in twelve years, you need to earn six percent (72 divided by 12 = 6).

Smart Ways to Save

Put your savings into secure investments. To eliminate risk, go to a credit union or bank with FDIC insurance. Start saving with:

1. **A money market account.**
   You typically earn higher interest on these than with a traditional savings account.

2. **A certificate of deposit, or CD.**
   A CD allows you to have a set interest rate for a predetermined period of time. The longer you lock in the interest rate, the higher it is. Be aware of penalties for early withdrawals.

3. **A money market mutual fund.**
   This is an investment in short-term bonds that provides a cash reserve for investors. It pays one to two percent more than a bank money market account, but it is not insured.

It's much more rewarding to earn interest on the money you're saving for future use than to spend 21 percent on interest payments. Imagine how much you could be earning if you took that 21 percent interest you pay each month and put it into savings.

Funding for Education

When we have a positive cash flow it is easier to help our children with their education. When a larger percentage of our income is no longer going to our mortgage or car payment it can go toward our desired education goals. We will not need to accumulate tens of thousands of dollars in education loans—or pay thousands more in interest on them!

Retirement Savings

It is no secret that we can no longer depend on Social Security, Medicare, Medicaid, or other government programs to provide for us when we retire. If these programs are in trouble *now,* no one can know for sure what will happen in the future. Yet it is difficult to save when we are stuck in the debt cycle. Becoming free of debt helps to ensure that we will have more saved up for our retirement.

There are more retirees today paying on their home mortgages than ever before. Recently we have seen more people in their sixties and seventies go back to work out of necessity. Some need to supplement their Social Security checks with extra income. Others realize a substantial loss on their investments and decide they need to work longer in order to make up the losses.

Business Ownership

Having our own small or part-time businesses gives us valuable experience in growing profitable businesses. We can still keep our daytime jobs and, at the same time, position ourselves to become more independent financially. Our home-grown business can become full-time once we have planned adequately for the transition.

Ending the *Debt Cycle*

One of the best financial advantages of debt-free living is learning to kick the credit habit. Choosing to pay off our short-term, then *long-term* debts, provides a welcome break from this cycle. Our family decided that being debt-free also included paying off our mortgage. Having no mortgage payments has allowed us to follow through with some of our life goals.

Spending our money wisely and cutting back on impulse spending becomes a satisfying and sufficient way of life. When we learn how to be smart spenders, it becomes second nature to us. Planning ahead for purchases and paying with cash rather than credit is financially freeing.

Psychological and Physiological Benefits

1. Better Communication

   When unpaid bills are no longer a preoccupation, communication improves between spouses, as well as among family members. There is less arguing and bickering. Our relationships improve at home and at work.

2. Contentment

   Those who have good money habits and plan well are more content all around. The saying, "Happiness is not having what you want, but wanting what you have," has a lot of truth to it. With the change of a few spending habits, we can learn to be content with what we have.

Jean Chatzky, a personal finance columnist, stated how she discovered in her research that managing money productively can make a person happier. English economist and researcher Andrew Oswald agreed.

"The ability to shape your own life, to control it, is very important. It's highly associated with psychological wellbeing,"[2] he said. Our ability to handle money responsibly creates more contentment.

3. More Confidence in the Future

We can plan for a comfortable future with simpler living today. Having a debt-free lifestyle also helps to eliminate the worries of what could happen tomorrow. I recall listening to a radio call-in program on finances a few years ago. The caller on the telephone was quite distraught.

"My wife and I just moved into a new home last year," he stated, "and I just found out I lost my job. What can I do?"

Before purchasing a new home, he could have asked himself, "Where do I stand financially? How would a new home purchase fit in with our future plans? If my wife or I lose a job, can we still afford our home payments?"

Although mortgage rates have been the lowest in about fifty years, house prices in most areas have continued to increase. Would owning a $300,000 home be affordable, taking other factors in the family budget into consideration?

Many families today have maxed out their budget with their house payments. They do not have any idea how their children will be able to afford a college education. They may hope to receive some government help or maybe a sports scholarship, but hoping is not planning.

When we have proactively planned for our future, we will be ready and able to face whatever the future may bring. Once we have little or no debt and a controlled lifestyle, we no longer need to fear the future.

4. A Calmer and Simpler Life

Psychologist and author Tim Kasser wrote that, "People who value money and image and status are actually less happy. We found this in people from age ten to eighty—all around the world." Kasser stated that those who weren't focused on fame, possessions, and fortune were happier with life and felt better overall. These people find that there are positive effects to the simpler life.[3]

Life becomes freeing when we can cut back on all that overwhelms us. As we pay off our financial obligations, we realize we can slow down our pace in life. We feel less rushed and more relaxed. We no longer feel we are in a rat race. Our lives become less complicated and demanding. As the bills become more manageable, life is simplified. We find we have more free time to do the things we enjoy.

John and his family are examples of those who have chosen to simplify their lives. John lives on a farm with his wife and five children. Although he lived in the city, John wanted a different lifestyle—one where he could be more self-sufficient. So he purchased a small farm, where he and his family grow most of their food. The children help with the chores. They own pigs, chickens, and cows. John explained his success with money management.

"When we were first married, I bought a $30,000 house, remodeled it, and sold it for a profit," he said. "I was also able to buy our second home for a reasonable price, fix that up, and sell *it* for a profit, as well. My wife and I have learned to live on a strict budget. So, when we purchased our farm we were able to deposit two-thirds of the total cost. We all enjoy our slower-paced lifestyle, including our children." When talking with John, you will find that he encourages others to live within their incomes, as well.

5. Less Stress

When there is little or no debt one's stress level is lowered considerably. Less stress and worry lead to better short-term and long-term health. Many people suffer poor health, not because of what they eat, but from what is *eating them*. They may have knots in their stomach and develop ulcers. "Type A" people tend to be more anxious and to develop anxiety-related problems. Having many credit obligations can easily multiply the anxiety. Individuals find that when financial matters are taken care of symptoms from health problems show immediate improvement.

Two decades ago *Time* magazine published an article about stress, entitled "Stress: Can We Cope?" It stated:

> The contemporary world is giving a lot of attention to stress. In the past thirty years, doctors and health officials have come to realize how heavy a toll stress is taking on the nation's wellbeing. According to the American Academy of Family Physicians, two-thirds of office visits to family doctors are prompted by stress-related symptoms. Stress is a major contributor, either directly or indirectly, to coronary heart disease, cancer, lung ailments, accidental injuries, cirrhosis of the liver and suicide.[4]

Since this article was written, we have seen many more evidences of stress in our society. When we have our finances under control, the stresses that we face every day are more manageable.

6. More Focused on Others

Being free of credit obligations enables us to help others more as we observe their needs. Previously, when we were caught up in all of our gadgets, bill payments, and frantic activities, we tended to develop an indifference to the needs of others. But as we become less concerned about ourselves, our hearts and minds become more focused outside ourselves. We have more time to volunteer. We are also able to give more to others and to worthy organizations. We may even discover new talents as we make contributions in others' lives. All of this makes us feel good about ourselves and about life. What a payoff for debt-free living!

7. Freedom to Change Careers

When we have no debt obligations, there is more freedom to change jobs or careers. A recent job satisfaction survey given to individuals ages twenty-five to fifty-four indicated that 38 percent of American workers are either somewhat dissatisfied or very dissatisfied with their jobs.[5]

When financial obligations are taken care of we are able to pursue other career interests with fewer concerns. For instance, I was able to make a career change after being in a career for more than twenty years, tapping into other abilities and interests of mine and following opportunities in those areas.

What other job or career interests do you have in mind? With proper planning, you may still have opportunity to pursue those interests.

Imagine the Possibilities!

There are many reasons to kick the credit habit. Consider *your* reasons. Take a moment to reflect on how your personal and family lives would be different today if you had no debt obligations. How would you spend your time differently? Consider your reasons and use them as a catalyst for creating your own financial freedom.

At the beginning of this chapter you listed your life goals. When you wrote down those goals, you were one step closer to completing them. Action leads to diligence, and a disciplined lifestyle opens up options and choices you never thought possible.

Those of us who achieve our objectives have a clear vision of what we want. We have a structured plan and yet remain flexible. We have the confidence to carry out our life goals. So can you.

Chapter Four

Where Do I Stand Financially?

"*You cannot keep out of trouble by spending more than you earn.*"

—Abraham Lincoln

Now we have identified the roadblocks that keep us from living more financially secure lives. Next we will focus on where we stand and where we are headed financially.

In the next several chapters we will learn how to:

1. **Deal with** the reasons why we are in debt.
2. **Determine** what our total indebtedness is.
3. **Discipline** ourselves as we follow through with our plans.

What are *Your* Lifestyle Priorities?

H. L. Hunt admits that he did not have a grade school or high school education. Yet that did not stop him from becoming a Texas oil billionaire. His words of advice are:

"Decide what you want. Decide what you are willing to exchange for it. Establish your priorities, and go to work."

What are your priorities? In numbers one to five, choose the statement that comes closest to your desires or behavior.

1. When it comes to automobiles, I like:

    a) the newest model available.
    b) dependable transportation.

2. I would like to live in a home that:

    a) is in a new neighborhood.
    b) comfortably fits our family's needs.

3. When I buy clothes:

    a) it doesn't matter how much they cost.
    b) I look for sales or bargains.

4. When I get a bonus check or extra money:

    a) I spend it on entertainment or recreation.
    b) I put it in my savings for future needs.

5. My miscellaneous expenses each month are usually:

    a) over two hundred dollars.
    b) under two hundred dollars.

If you answered with three or more "a" statements, you probably spend more than you earn and make decisions based mostly on your emotions.

If you answered with three or more "b" statements, you try to be a more responsible consumer and you see the need to have resources set aside for future necessities.

A basic concept in economics is *needs vs. wants*. It is the "wants" part that tends to get people into trouble financially. There's nothing wrong with having "wants" as long as they don't get in the way of a family's basic needs. Unfortunately, some people think that prosperity is that wonderful time when they can always get enough credit to live beyond their means!

Is your lifestyle reasonable and balanced or is it like the tower of Pisa, slightly off balance? You may think your income is not that large. However, realize that compared to people in other areas of the world, the average American is in the top five percent in wage-earnings. Consider how you rate in the areas of spending for food, clothing, and housing. First, look at your monthly income and expenses.

☒ Track Your Spending for a Month

Record all of your spending for one month. (Worksheet One is provided for recording your everyday expenses.) Both husband and wife can keep an itemized record or diary, and then combine both records for a more accurate look at expenditures. Write down every purchase in order to know the actual dollar amount you've spent. Keep your checkbook balanced each month. This helps your recordkeeping go more smoothly and eliminates costly fees for overdrafts.

Keep your receipts in order to get an accurate dollar amount for recording your purchases on the *Monthly Expenses Worksheet* (Worksheet One). Keep receipts for credit and debit transactions, as well as cash purchases. Remember to enter the debit card purchases in your checkbook ledger as soon as possible.

Sample 1

Monthly Expenses Worksheet

Name: Steve and Jill
Month: March 31

Monthly Spending - Page 1

Income	Giving	Home Mtg./Ins.	Repairs/Maint./Furniture	Property Taxes	Water	Sani-tation	Electric	Gas/Htg.	Cable	Phone/Cell/Internet	Groceries/School Lunches	School Tuition/Daycare	Misc.	Entermt./Eating Out	Total
995	50	800	50	150	35	25	60	60	40	80	60		20	10	
605	100	100								50	30		25	10	
995											25		40	40	
605											120		25	25	
											45		15	40	
											40		30	35	
											60		10	40	
											100			20	
											60				
3200	150	900	50	150	35	25	60	60	40	130	540		165	220	
															2,375

Column Totals   Total - p. 1

Monthly Spending - Page 2

Gas	Car Loans	Car Rprs.	Ins. & Plates	Doctors/Dentist	Prescrip-tions	Medical Insurance	Assoc. & Clubs	Clothes	Emerg. Fund	Savings/Invest.	Life Ins.	Vacation	Credit Oblig.	Total Pg. 1	Total Pg. 2
25	125	50	200	55	60	250	30	15	50		70		100		
15	150			30			60	15					100		
15				50				30							
15								40							
70	275	50	200	135	60	250	90	100	50	0	70		200		
														2,375	1,550
															3,925

Column Totals   Expenses Total

☒ **Observe Your Spending Patterns**

It is important to be aware of your spending patterns before you come up with a new monthly budget. As you begin to do so, you will be more successful in reducing your expenses.

As Jill tracked her spending on the *Monthly Expenses Worksheet* she found that she spent more on groceries, 1) when she was hungry and, 2) when she brought her children along to the store. She also realized that she bought more junk food when she shopped later in the day.

Steve noted that he had been eating his lunches at restaurants an average of three times a week. He found that he tended to spend much more on entertainment on Saturdays, his golfing day.

Take another look at Sample 1. Note the following:

- In the month of March, Steve and Jill earned a net total of $3,200.
- They spent $1,440 for housing, groceries, and school lunches.
- They spent $385 on miscellaneous, entertainment, and eating out.
- They set aside a total of $50 for their emergency fund.
- Their monthly credit obligations add up to $1,375 ($900 for home mortgage, $275 for car loans, and $200 for credit cards).

1. Evaluate Your Spending Patterns

    After you record your expenses for a month (See Worksheet One), take an objective look at how much you spent. Compare your income and outgo for the month:

- What was your monthly income?
- How much did you spend for housing and food?
- Are you building up an emergency fund? How much are you setting aside for savings?
- What percentage of your income went to credit obligations?
- How much did you spend on entertainment and miscellaneous items?

Time to Get Organized

In order to get an accurate picture of your family's yearly spending it is vital to have the necessary records available. Sometimes our *estimates* are way off the mark.

Developing an efficient system of organization for your records saves you time, money, and frustration. Develop an efficient system for organizing your bills, receipts, and important papers. Set up filing systems for your insurance policies, tax records, brokerage accounts, bills, and receipts. If your system of organizing is paper piles A, B, C, and so forth, you will need to reconsider having a more efficient system. You may know where everything is, but does your spouse? Would he or she be able to locate an important piece of information quickly?

When my parents moved to an assisted living center, I organized their important papers and records. I was grateful that my mother had previously labeled her file folders and other records. That made my job much easier. I purchased a few storage crates, a box of hanging file folders, and a box of manila folders. I narrowed down the paperwork and kept those items that were most current and important.

What could have taken days to accomplish I did in one afternoon.

As you organize your papers, divide them into three groups. Decide what you will keep, shred, or throw out. It is best to shred credit card solicitations and personal information in order to protect yourself from identity theft.

A great way to start organizing your papers is with an accordion-style file folder. Your current financial papers should be kept in one location for easy access. Records that are no longer current can be kept in a separate file and safely placed in storage.

I keep my investment statements in three-ring binders. One binder is for my brokerage account. The other binders are for mutual fund investments, including my IRA and 403B accounts. This helps me easily assess the changes in my accounts from year to year.

Keep a current list of your safe-deposit box contents. Cross items you remove from the box off your list. Add new items stored there to your list. Keep your safe-deposit key with your records.

The following chart will help you decide what papers to keep, where to keep them, and for how long.

Recordkeeping

Document	Where to Keep	How Long
Canceled checks and bank statements; Records of itemized deductions (interest, medical, etc.)	Current file Storage	One year Five years
Contracts	Safe-deposit box and lawyer	Until expiration
Household inventory	Safe-deposit box and current file	Keep up-to-date

Insurance policies	Current file	Indefinitely
Loans and promissory notes	Current file	Until paid off
Medical records	Current file	Keep up-to-date
Mortgage records; Home-improvement receipts	Safe-deposit box, current file	As long as you own home
Net worth statements	Current file	Indefinitely
Personal records (birth certificates, marriage/divorce papers, military service)	Safe-deposit box	Indefinitely
Real estate deeds	Safe-deposit box	Until property is sold
Receipts for major purchases	Current file	As long as owned
Stock or bond certificates	Safe-deposit box or broker	Until sold
Tax returns	Current file Storage	Three years Three years or more
Vehicle titles	Safe-deposit box	Until vehicle is sold
Warranties	Current file	Until expiration
Will	Safe-deposit box and lawyer	Indefinitely

—*The Consumer Reports Money Book*[1]

Look at Your Expenditures

Once you have kept a record of your family expenses for a month, fill out the *Monthly Income and Expenses Summary* (Worksheet Two). This is a summary of how you spend your money throughout the year.

Remember to factor in the variable expenses. Use readily available records for variable expenses such as:

- home repairs and maintenance
- gasoline and car repairs
- health insurance and health costs
- natural gas and electricity
- phone expenses (home, cell)
- food
- child care

This provides a more accurate amount of the money you've spent during an average month.

In Sample 2 of the Monthly Income and Expenses Summary, we note that Steve and Jill first recorded their individual and combined gross incomes. Next, they listed their charitable giving amounts and monthly taxes.

Their combined spendable income was $3,200 per month, after subtracting charitable giving and taxes.

Sample 2

Monthly Income and Expenses Summary

	Steve's Monthly Income	Jill's Monthly Income
Income:		
Salary	$ 2600	$ 1500
Annuities or Trusts		
Interest and Dividend Income	50	
Pension and Retirement Income		
Government Benefits		
Rental Income		
Social Security Income		
Child Support Income		100
Other Income		
Total Gross Income	$ 2650	$ 1600

Steve's and Jill's Combined Gross Income: $ 4250

		Steve	Jill
Expenses:			
1.	**Charitable Giving**	$ 100	$ 50
2.	**Taxes**		
	Federal Income Tax	300	150
	State Tax	50	50
	Local Tax	30	20
	Social Security Tax	150	100
	Medicare Tax	30	20
	Total Taxes	$ 560	$ 340
	Total Giving & Taxes	$ 660	$ 390
	Net Spendable Income:	$ 1990	$ 1210

(Total gross income less giving and taxes)

Steve's and Jill's Combined Spendable Income: $ 3,200

Where Do I Stand Financially?

Combined Monthly Expenses

3. **Housing**

Mortgage/Rent	$ 800
Homeowner's Insurance	$ 100
Property Taxes	$ 150
Gas/Heating	$ 100
Electricity	$ 50
Water	$ 35
Sanitation	$ 25
Telephone/Internet	$ 100
Cellular Phone	$ 50
Cable	$ 40
Maintenance/Repairs	$ 50
Furnishings	$ 30
Other	$
Total Housing	$ 1530

4. **Transportation**

Auto Loans	$ 275
Car Insurance	$ 150
License Plates	$ 50
Maintenance/Repairs	$ 100
Gas	$ 100
Parking/Tolls	$ 40
AAA Fees	$ 35
Total Auto	$ 750

5. **Food**

Groceries	$ 480
School Lunches	$ 60
Total Food	$ 540

6. **Insurance**

Medical Insurance	$ 250
Dental Insurance	$ 30
Life Insurance	$ 70
Other	$
Total Insurance	$ 350

7. **Health Expenses**

Doctor	$ 55
Dentist/Orthodontist	$ 100
Prescriptions/Vitamins	$ 60
Optometrist/Glasses	$ 50

Health Club	$ 60
Total Health	$ 325

8. Entertainment

Eating Out	$ 100
Movies/Game Rentals	$ 40
Babysitting	$
Club Fees/Camp	$
Magazines/Newspapers	$ 40
Books	$ 20
Computer Games and Software	$ 60
Other	$
Total Entertainment	$ 260

9. Clothing/Shoes — $ 200

10. School Tuition/Daycare — $

11. Miscellaneous

Toiletries, Household	$ 50
Dry Cleaning	$ 25
Hair Care/Grooming Supplies	$ 40
Stamps, mailings	$ 15
Gifts/Flowers	$ 25
Allowances	$ 40
Pet Care	$
Other	$ 30
Total Miscellaneous	$ 225

12. Debt

Credit Cards	$ 100
Loans	$ 100
Other	$
Total Debts Payments	$ 200

13. Vacation — $ 80

14. Savings

Emergency Fund	$ 50
401K	$
IRA	$
College Savings	$
Other	$
Other	$
Other	$

Total Savings	$ 50
Total Living Expenses	**$ 4,510**
Cash Flow Margin	**$ (1,310)**

(Net spendable income, minus living expenses)

As you look at Sample 2 you will note that Steve and Jill have a *negative cash flow*. In other words, their living expenses added up to more than their income. The first thing they need to do is look for some areas in which to lower their spending each month.

Look at the numbers on your *Monthly Income and Expenses Summary* (Worksheet Two). Do you have a reasonable cash flow margin? In what areas can you cut costs? Make a commitment to change your spending habits wherever necessary or the situation will worsen.

What can you do to accomplish those more important goals? How can you make the best use of your resources? The authors of *The Millionaire Next Door* wrote: "Being frugal is the cornerstone of wealth-building."[2] It's not how much you make; rather, it's how much you keep!

Determine Your Spending Objectives

Your new budget needs to be realistic in order for it to work. Decide just how much you are willing to cut back on monthly expenses. Estimate the dollar amount that can be redirected for debt repayment. Once you know where you tend to spend irresponsibly and get off course, the budget you plan for yourself can become a road map that will give you more confidence as you head in the right direction.

Having more money is not the answer. Many people assume their money problems come from not earning enough. This issue is not so much that they *cannot* live on their income, but that they *will not* live on it. Disciplined use of your money is the key. Where there is discipline, you accept the inconveniences today for the rewards tomorrow.

The statement, "People don't plan to fail, they fail to plan," has a lot of truth to it. Too many individuals starting out on their own begin not knowing how they will pay their bills. They don't know how they will afford the new house they purchased or apartment they are renting. They are content to live one month at a time. To thrive financially it is vital to take time to plan ahead.

Dr. Viktor Frankl, Professor of Psychiatry, University of Vienna, said this: "The last of the human freedoms (is) to choose one's attitude in any given set of circumstances, to choose one's own ways." As you reflect on your life, be aware of the choices you have made. Although some circumstances are predetermined, accept responsibility for what you *can* change. If you don't, things won't get any better. Acknowledge what you need to change in order to make it better—then take the leap and do it!

Chapter Five

Steps for Getting on the Right Track

"*The way you get rid of a habit is you coax it down the stairs one step at a time.*"

—Mark Twain

Some people look at their failures and stop there. They don't realize they can use their failures for personal growth. Their mistakes can be stepping-stones in their lives.

To move ahead, believe in yourself and believe that you can succeed. If you fear things won't work out, you will continue to feed your fears. You no longer need to hold on to doubt and discouragement. When you believe something *can* be done, your mind will work for you and help you find ways to do it.

The Four-Step Plan to Positive Cash Flow

Would you like to reduce or eliminate debt? Here are four basic steps to follow:

☒ Define clearly *why* you went into debt.
☒ Remember to *spend less* than you earn.
☒ Develop a *realistic* payment plan.
☒ Set *long-term goals* for a long-term perspective.

Define Clearly Why You Went Into Debt

In Chapter Two we looked at roadblocks to a debt-free lifestyle. We examined the ways in which we easily get caught up in the debt cycle. Refer to those reasons and determine which ones have caused you to spend more than you earned.

How can you keep this from happening on a continual basis? If you always do what you've always done, you'll always get what you've always gotten.

Instead, make a list of possible solutions to help solve the problem, then decide which ones you will use to remedy your situation. Your solutions may include making and implementing some tough decisions. When we change our way of thinking and our belief systems, we impact our level of success.

Don't expect any quick fixes for a poor credit history. Those companies that advertise credit repair services cannot remove your credit history's data. Only you can repair your credit. You will need to contact each creditor and work with them on a realistic payment plan.

Theoretically, credit card balances should be paid in full at the end of each month. If they are not paid in full, we should attempt to pay them off within the next few months. Too many of us have learned to trust our credit cards to get us through crunch times. When we receive unsolicited credit card applications in the mail, it is OK to shred them!

Bob and Jan struggled to find the right approach for handling their spending money. Both agreed that Bob is better at handling finances, so Bob gave his wife Jan what he thought was a reasonable amount of spending cash each week. This money was not for bills but merely for entertainment. Jan complained that by the middle of the week she had no money left.

Looking for a better solution, Bob told Jan she could use their joint checkbook for her expenses and miscellaneous items. However, that did not work well, either, since several of the checks she wrote bounced. Rather than go back to the cash system, where there is a limited amount of money to spend, Jan used the couple's credit cards. This was a big mistake. She did not have control over her spending habits and ran up thousands of dollars on the cards. Jan had an emotional need to spend, which led to serious financial problems and consequences for the family.

Remember to Spend Less Than You Earn

We all know how learned behaviors are hard to overcome. Yet it *is* possible to live within your means and develop a disciplined lifestyle. *How?* A personal spending plan is necessary for gaining control of your finances. You can control the results tomorrow by how you live now.

Reducing lifestyle consumption does not come easily to many individuals. However, the money that is freed up from nonessential and unplanned purchases can help to balance your budget. It can also go toward your debt repayment plan and savings plan.

Those who accumulate wealth are those who can control cash flow. Remember that the direction we are facing determines our destination. We are either walking in the direction of accumulating more debt or in the direction of

85

having a positive cash flow. Cutting lifestyle consumption can help generate immediate cash flow.

Develop a Realistic Payment Plan

If you are in a tough financial situation it is likely that it took several years for you to get there. Don't expect everything to be resolved in several months—or even in a year. Plan to take the same amount of time to get out of your money troubles as it took you to get into them. The process can be speeded up, however, if you have an aggressive plan. Your new monthly spending plan is a work in progress. It will take time to get to where you want to be financially.

Making a budget is not hard to do. It is much like making any other plans. What *is* essential is making a commitment to follow through with it. Be committed to your plan. The more committed you are, the sooner you will see your rewards. Be accountable to someone on how well you are sticking to your budget. You could be accountable to a spouse or a friend.

If you need help resolving financial problems, you could contact a credit counselor.

GreenPath Debt Solutions is a reputable nonprofit credit counseling agency. It is formerly known as Consumer Credit Counseling Service. The organization is a member of the National Foundation for Credit Counseling (NFCC) and the Better Business Bureau. For more information, call 866-648-8122 or visit GreenPath's website at www.greenpath.com.[1]

Keep in mind how your values and priorities affect your decisions in life. When you have come to the crossroads of decisions, you should have your goals firmly in mind.

Set Long-Term Goals for Gaining a Long-Term Perspective

Motivational speaker Paul J. Meyer stated that over 30 percent of people have never decided what they really want out of life. They are just getting by. They don't even have short-range goals, such as the next promotion. Each of us should be able to clearly define our goals—from our daily goals to our lifetime goals. These tie in with our financial goals. Meyer lists the five basic factors to consider in setting a goal:

- ☒ It needs to be your *own* personal goal.
- ☒ It needs to be stated *positively*.
- ☒ It needs to be *specific* and written.
- ☒ It needs to be *realistic, compatible,* and *attainable*.
- ☒ Certain basic personality characteristics need to be included.

These goals must be defined and measured. The clearer your goals are, the more effective you will be in attaining them. Look beyond the now and project into the future as you imagine what your life could be like. Ask yourself, "What am I going to do this week, month, and year to attain my goals?"

Long-term goals can include things like: saving for college and retirement, paying off your mortgage, or starting a business. Your retirement savings would depend on your age and your income. Paying off your mortgage as quickly as possible can save you thousands of dollars in the long term and give you much more flexibility in the future.

It is important to build up an emergency fund, whether you think you can afford it or not. This provides an extra cushion when things do not go as planned. One can never know for sure when a job loss or illness will occur. Rather than taking out a loan or using your credit card, you will be able to take the money from your personal emergency fund when these things occur.

Make steady savings a priority. Begin by saving 10 percent of your income. It is necessary to have a disciplined savings plan. If we save nothing, we will earn nothing.

Charles Kettering, General Motors Vice President and Manager of Research, did not focus on impossibilities. He admired those who pushed the limits.

"The Wright brothers flew right through the smoke screen of impossibility," he stated. It may seem impossible at first to save anything, but if we get beyond what seems like our limiting factors, we can do it.

Make It a Partnership

When two people marry they bring their beliefs, experiences, and spending habits into the relationship. They also bring their personal dreams for the future.

Laura was attracted to her husband because he didn't hesitate to spend generously on her when they were dating. He was full of adventure and was a lot of fun to be around. He bought things impulsively, surprising her from time to time.

However, once they were married his impulsive ways of spending began to grate on her and caused friction in the relationship. Laura did not know from one month to the next where their money was going, and some of it seemed to be "missing." She and her husband could not keep track of their expenses. That made it even more difficult to plan together. What she thought she liked about him turned out to be something that caused discord between them.

Miscommunication results from different assumptions. We enter marriage with our own ideas of how we can or should handle the money. As couples, we can't expect to agree on everything; that is understandable. However, we can strive together to have a working relationship and partnership. The first few years of marriage are probably the most difficult ones for creating a workable plan of money management.

In order to make changes in the way your family handles money, there needs to be cooperation in the household. When creating your spending plan, do not make it one-sided. It should be planned by both of you and *for* both of you. Knowing where you stand and planning together frees you both up. Planning with your spouse not only facilitates more fairness in the decision-making, but the process of shared thinking also multiplies the possibilities for positive change.

A husband and wife need to have honest and open discussions. When they use their strengths and work together as partners there is balance in the decision-making.

Budget Basics

A monthly budget tells us:

1. Where our money is coming from and where it is going.
2. How much is coming in and how much is going out.

A budget is a powerful way to manage money. Having a budget will help you control miscellaneous spending. It serves as a *reality check* and shows where your spending is excessive. Budgeting helps balance spending with income.

A budget is simply a financial yearly plan divided by twelve. It includes *all* spending. Items that come due quarterly, semi-annually, or annually are factored in. This includes life and health insurance, dental and medical bills, vacations, auto repairs, and taxes. Each item is realistically included so that when those predicted expenses come due, the amount is already set aside.

Helpful Tips for Creating Cash Flow

In what ways can we cut costs? Consider the following areas:

- Start with the housing expense. Evaluate how cost can be lowered.

- Consider your transportation expenses. Is your monthly car payment or car insurance affordable?

- See if there are ways you can cut your grocery bill. You can shop from a list, shop alone, look for weekly discounts, or limit the number of visits to the grocery store.

- Look at your entertainment and miscellaneous expenses. Costs for dining out can easily add up for a family. When you add soft drinks for everyone, the total can be more than expected. Try ordering water instead of soft drinks. Draw names for gift exchanges. What about eliminating the purchase of subscriptions to magazines you don't have time to read or are no longer interested in reading?

- Examine your clothing and shoe purchases. Can you live with what you have for a while? Consider buying your clothing where and when there are sales.

- Work-related expenses can be reduced. Bringing a lunch from home instead of eating out every day could be a solution. Buying new clothes for work on a regular basis won't help your pocketbook or your budget, either.

- Do you have checking fees and charges? Find a low-cost or free checking account.

- You may have assets that can be liquidated. Cash in your savings bonds.

- Go through your house and make a list of what you could sell in a newspaper classified ad or garage sale. Check the attic, basement, and garage. When you advertise in a newspaper, be specific. For smaller items, you can plan on a well-organized garage sale. You probably have more assets sitting idle than you realize. Turn these into cash.

- Think of sources from which you can begin building up your saving accounts. When you receive a bonus or a birthday check, put that in your savings account. Many people take their tax check and look for ways to spend it rather than using it as a great source of income for savings.

Remember that management of cash flow is basic to making your budget work well. Do not doubt your ability to become free of debt. Remain focused on your goals and financial plans. Look for ways to continue improving your financial skills.

Analyze Your Budget

Refer to the *Monthly Income and Expenses Summary* (Worksheet Two). Transfer the income and total category amounts to the "Existing Budget" column on the *Budget Analysis* (Worksheet Three).

Observe Steve and Jill's Budget Analysis. According to their budget record, they are spending about $1,300 more than they are making during the average month. They will need to cut down considerably in order to bring their income and expenses into balance.

Below, they have listed the changes they will need to make in order to follow through with their new budget. For example, they have decided to sell a car, to eat out less, and to lower their grocery bills.

Sample 3

Budget Analysis

Name: *Steve and Jill*

Date: *March 31*

Total Income Per Year: $51,000   Gross Income Per Month: $4,250
Net Spendable Income Per Month: $3,200

Monthly Expenses	Existing Budget	New Proposed Budget	Action Plan
1. Charitable Giving	$ 150	$ 150	
2. Taxes	$ 900	$ 900	

Net Spendable Income	$ 3,200	$ 3,200	
3. Housing	$ 1,530	$ 1,300	Rent out room above garage. Lower heat.
4. Transportation	$ 750	$ 400	Sell one car. Teens help pay for gas.
5. Food	$ 540	$ 360	Pack sack lunches. Buy less processed food.
6. Insurance	$ 350	$ 350	
7. Health Expenses	$ 325	$ 210	
8. Entertainment	$ 260	$ 100	Get videos at library. Eat out less.
9. Clothing/Shoes	$ 200	$ 100	Limit spending for each person.
10. School Tuition/Daycare	$	$	
11. Miscellaneous	$ 225	$ 100	Home haircuts for guys. Limit dry cleaning.
12. Debts	$ 200	$ 200	
13. Vacations	$ 80	$ 30	Vacation closer to home.
14. Savings	$ 50	$ 50	
Total Living Expenses	$4,510	$ 3,200	
Cash Flow Margin = Income/Expenses	$ (1,310)	$ 0	

Once you decide the budget changes you want to make, write those figures in the "New Proposed Budget" column. List the changes you will need to make in order to follow through with your proposed budget.

Net Worth

Steve and Jill have determined their net worth by completing a *Net Worth Worksheet* (Sample 4). Note that Steve and Jill's total assets are $152,500 and their total liabilities are $124,000. That leaves them with a positive net worth of $28,500. Their credit card debt totals $10,000. Their home is valued at $120,000, yet they still owe $100,000 on it.

Sample 4

Net Worth Worksheet

Name: *Steve and Jill*

Date: *March 31*

Assets

Bank/Credit Union

Cash/Checking Accounts	$ 1,000
Savings Accounts	$ 1,500
Money Market Funds	$ 3,000
Certificates of Deposit	$ 2,500

Investments

Stocks and Bonds	$ 2,000
Mutual Funds	$ 1,000
Other	$
Other	$
Life Insurance: Cash Value	$ 1,000
Company Pensions: Cash Value	$

Real Estate

Home	$ 120,000
Rentals	$
Other Real Estate	$

Vehicles

Auto #1	$ 8,000
Auto #2	$ 8,000
Furniture and Appliances	$ 3,000
Jewelry	$ 1,000
Collectibles	$ 500
Other	$
Total Assets	$ 152,500

Liabilities

Credit Cards	$ 10,000

Auto Loans	$ 8,000
Bank Loans	$
Student Loans	$ 6,000
Equity Loans	$
Personal Loans	$
Mortgage(s)	$ 100,000
Other	$
Total Liabilities	$ 124,000
Net Worth	$ 28,500

(Net Worth = Total Assets/Total Liabilities)

Now that you have worked on your financial plan to have a positive cash flow (Worksheet Three), complete Worksheet Four. This summary helps you evaluate your assets (what you own) and liabilities (what you owe). Examples of *assets* are: personal property, residences (other real estate), annuities, pensions, IRA accounts, mutual funds, stocks and bonds, certificates of deposit, money market funds, savings accounts, cash, and checking accounts.

Examples of *liabilities* are: unpaid taxes, credit cards, loans (bank, auto, boat), and home mortgages. If you have not calculated your net worth before, you will need to gather your most recent information on the following:

1. Credit Union or Bank Statements
2. Credit Card Statements
3. Investment Account Statements
4. Pension Account Statements
5. Retirement Savings Account Statements
6. Car or Other Loan Statements
7. Student Loan Statements
8. Mortgage Statements
9. Cash Value Life Insurance Statement
10. An Itemized Listing of Your Properties and Valuables

On Determining Asset Value

   A. Life Insurance.

   Cash value is not the same as the *benefit amount.* Only list the cash value of your policies.

   B. Car or Home Values.

   If you are unsure of the value of your car or home, determine what the *fair market value* would be. This would be what you would probably be able to sell the items for today.

Now that you have completed the *Net Worth Worksheet* (Worksheet Four), note what your net value is today in dollars. By beginning to calculate your net worth now you will be able to measure the growth of your assets as you whittle down your liabilities. You will most likely find positive change. Once you begin this process, you will find that it is not that complicated.

Walk in the Right Direction

As we become aware of where our money goes (and where it no longer goes), we become wise consumers. Now that we are headed in the right direction financially we should not wonder if it is OK to get another loan. Don't take on any new debt. If you do, you will be turning your back on financial freedom. Remember, you are either moving ahead or backward.

Let's take a look again at the four steps to positive cash flow. They are:

1. Define clearly *why* you went into debt.
2. Remember to *spend less* than you earn.
3. Develop a *realistic* payment plan.
4. Set *long-term goals* for a long-term perspective.

In this chapter, we have asked ourselves the reasons why we overspend, what we can do to control our spending, and how we can create more cash flow.

We know that it is not how much we *make* that is important, but *how much we have left*. In the next chapter we will look at how you can develop a plan to manage your finances wisely.

Chapter Six

Develop a Manageable Plan

"The biggest decisions in life are emotionally made and then intellectually justified, not vice versa."
—Howard Calhoun

You have probably learned by now that if *you* do not make plans for your money, others will. Others will tell you or sell you *their* plans for your money, but stick with your plan! When you begin to think confidently, you will act confidently, so set your goals high. This will give you a vision of a promising future.

Get Ready to Reduce Your Credit Obligations

You have looked at your spending habits and considered ways to get moving—and get out of the debt cycle. Now, once you have calculated what you need to live on, determine how much of the remaining money can go to creditors. Let's look at one example of this.

Get Set to Develop a Plan of Action for Reducing Debts

Steve and Jill have listed their monthly loan obligations and liabilities in Sample 5. Note the interest rates listed in descending order. Their credit cards have the highest interest rates, then the auto loans, the home mortgage, and the student loans. They need to begin paying off the credit card with the highest rate first.

Sample 5

Debt Repayment Plan

Name: *Steve and Jill*

Date: _____

	Balance Owed	Projected Interest Rate (%)	Monthly Payment	Date of Last Payment
Credit card: Visa	$ 4,000	18	40	
Credit card: MasterCard	$ 6,000	16	60	
Credit card: Discover Card	$			
Credit card: Department store	$			
Credit Card	$			
Credit Card	$			
Auto Loans	$ 8,000	9	150	
Bank/Credit Union Loans	$			
Student Loans	$ 6,000	4	100	
Equity Loans	$			
Personal Loans	$			
Home Mortgage	$ 100,000	8	900	
Other	$			

Other	$	
Total Amount Owed	**$ 124,000**	1,250

Once you begin to balance your budget, plan to have some of the extra money go toward your debt reduction. Refer to the Liabilities section of your *Net Worth Worksheet* (Worksheet Four), if necessary, for current figures. Complete the *Debt Repayment Plan* (Worksheet Five).

List any longstanding financial loans you have. These may include:

1. Credit Card Bills
2. Auto Loans
3. Installment Loans
4. Boat Loans
5. RV Loans
6. School Loans
7. Loans from Friends or Relatives
8. Mortgage Loans

Tackle Those Credit Obligations

Paying off credit cards should be a top priority since paying high interest rates helps the bank, not you. It would take years to pay off your credit cards if all you did was make the minimum payment on a loan. Instead, as you pay each one off, take that "extra" money and put it down on the next loan you intend to pay off.

When additional money becomes available, use it to speed up your debt repayment plan.

You will see the number of credit obligations be eliminated much more quickly and this will motivate you even more to continue.

Control Your Consumer Debt

Control your credit card and consumer debt by limiting the number of cards you have. Decide which one or two major credit cards you want to keep, then cancel and cut apart the others. Do not hinder your progress by signing up for any new credit cards.

Make it a habit to pay with cash, not credit. After all, you can still pay with dollar bills, checks, or debit cards. Unfortunately, even fast food advertisers are telling us we can charge a hamburger on our credit cards.

You might consider using your credit card as emergency cash only. When I travel, my card does come in handy. I can rent a car, reserve a hotel room, or purchase airplane tickets over the phone. As soon as the bill arrives, though, I make sure to pay the full card balance.

A great goal for homeowners is to accelerate the mortgage payments in order to retire the debt as soon as possible. This is especially true for individuals in their retirement years.

As we become more financially literate, we can free ourselves of the loans we have by becoming knowledgeable about money management by reading books and magazines. The more we know, the less we will need to depend on others and their services and the less likely we will be to fall for bad advice or bad deals.

Keep Accurate Records

It is essential to have accurate financial records. Learn how to balance a checkbook. I once read of a finance counselor who discovered that fewer than two of ten couples knew how to keep their checkbook balanced. Carefully record each check in the ledger. If you use a debit card, immediately enter the purchase in your checkbook ledger. Don't invite overdraft charges on checks written with insufficient funds.

It is important for you to establish spending goals with your spouse. If you establish them together, you will most likely follow them. Divide the responsibilities for payments between both of you if this is feasible. For example, the husband pays the mortgage, life, homeowner's, and car insurance payments, property taxes, and private school tuition. The wife is responsible for groceries, utilities, water, telephone bills, and other monthly expenses.

Some couples prefer to have a joint checkbook, while others like to have separate checkbooks. Whichever way you choose, it is important to see that the system ensures the bills are paid on time and that accurate records are kept. Doing this helps to eliminate communication problems.

Be aware of your billing cycles and follow up with creditors if your bills should not arrive on time. Mail the bill payments immediately after writing them, preferably at the post office. This helps to prevent mail theft. If you decide to use an Internet bill pay system with your credit union or bank, have an organized system for paying your bills.

It serves no benefit to develop a plan if you do not put it into action. If you find yourself taking a detour from your spending plan or financial goals, you need to immediately ask yourself *why* you made those unplanned purchases and quickly correct course.

Manage Money More Easily

Here are some ways to help your payment and savings systems run more smoothly:

☒ Set aside money into your savings before paying the bills.

☒ If your employer has a payroll savings plan, use payroll deduction for 401K savings plans or insurance plans.

☒ Pay your insurance premiums using an automatic checking withdrawal system. Make sure you enter the amount withdrawn on the first of each month so the amount is properly accounted for.

☒ Have a direct deposit system set up with your credit union or bank. Direct allocated amounts to your checking, emergency fund, college fund, or other savings. This saves you time by not having to stand in line to cash your paycheck. You will also be more likely to save money by not spending what you might regard as *extra* cash.

Develop a Plan of Action for Keeping within Your Budget

Develop a plan that is manageable and realistic. This will make it easier to stay with the planned budget.

Consider the following target allocations:

* 10% charitable giving
* 10% life insurance, savings, and investments

- 10% emergency fund
- 70% current expenses

Consider how you might be able to adjust your spending in the following areas:

1. Lifestyle
2. Food
3. Clothes
4. Utilities
5. Entertainment
6. Gifts
7. Insurance

1. Lifestyle

Many couples buy homes based on two incomes. Even then they may be talked into buying a house that surpasses a reasonable mortgage payment limit. When other home expenses, such as homeowner's insurance, utilities, and maintenance are factored in, the total cost quickly adds up to too much.

Decide whether your home expenses can be reduced in any way. For instance, an alternative to always buying new furniture and appliances is buying good-quality used items.

Examine your choices of activities and your possessions. Look at how you can you refine your lifestyle choices in order to create more cash flow. Before spending money, you might ask yourself, "How many hours of my day did I work so I could pay for this? Is that a fair exchange?"

2. Food

    Grocery expenses can consume a large part of one's budget. Tips for spending less are:

    -   Plan meal menus ahead for the coming month or week.

    -   Buy from a list. Keep the list in the kitchen where you can add items as needed.

    -   Save by not purchasing as many soft drinks, snacks, prepackaged and processed foods.

    -   When purchasing groceries, look for those brands that are on sale or discounted that week.

    -   Do not go grocery shopping when you are hungry or stressed.

    -   Shop alone. This usually reduces your shopping time and the number of items you will purchase.

3. Clothing

    Clothing purchases should be budgeted. The source of conflict among family members tends not so much to be the item of clothing, but the *cost* of the item.

Look for clothes of good quality.

Comparison shop and take advantage of seasonal sales.

Many families charge clothing on their department store credit cards. Avoid these cards, since the small discounts you get when you sign up are quickly eaten up by the higher interest rates on the card.

- Keep your credit cards at home when you shop for clothes. You will save by paying cash for clothes.

4. Utilities

My father jokingly called our utility bills "futility bills." There is no doubt that we appreciate having heat and electricity. However, there are ways you can reduce this expense.

If your utility bills vary greatly throughout the year, setting up a budget plan with your utility company is a great alternative. That way, you can know exactly how much you will pay each month for utilities.

- Check to see that your home is properly insulated. Insulating the attic helps cut energy costs.

- Have good storm windows.

- Cut down on energy use whenever possible.

5. Entertainment

> This category includes eating out, sporting events, movies, and clubs. One can easily overspend here. Those who eat out often will find that they can save considerable money by limiting their meals eaten out of the home. When you do eat out, you can save by going out for lunch instead of dinner.
> We can save on entertainment costs by checking out videos, CDs, DVDs, and books at the library.

6. Gifts

> We may think we don't spend that much on gifts, but if we were to add up the cost for birthdays, anniversaries, Christmas, baby and shower gifts, we may be surprised. Consider these ways to save on gift-giving:
>
> Plan ahead for special occasions. Buy items when they are on sale. You can find many items discounted by as much as 50 percent or more during holiday seasons. Try these strategies, as well:
>
> - Make some of your gifts.
> - Draw names for gift exchanges.
> - Keep from buying gifts on credit.

7. Insurance (Health, Homeowner's, Life, Auto)

  a. Health Insurance

> It is best not to drop your health insurance payments. If possible, choose a plan with a higher deductible.

Remember that if you can't easily afford the monthly payments, you most likely won't be able to handle a large, unexpected medical bill for emergency surgery or a long hospital stay.

Your employer probably offers health insurance, which provides group rates. These are usually less expensive than health insurance rates when purchased individually.

If you need to purchase your own insurance, contact Quotesmith at *www.quotesmith.com*. They provide information on health care plans. And remember, you pay lower monthly fees with higher co-payments and deductibles. It is important that your health insurance policy cover preventative care. Ask about pre-existing health conditions. Some insurers won't cover these health problems; others may wait for a period of time before covering these costs.

b. Homeowner's Insurance

There are ways you can lower your homeowner's insurance bill. *Money* magazine lists ten ways to do this:

- **Comparison shop.** Get quotes from at least three companies. Check with the National Association of Insurance Commissioners (naic.org) for any complaints recorded.

- **Know your house's claims history.** Your CLUE (Comprehensive Loss Underwriting

Exchange) report can be ordered at www.
choicetrust.com for a fee. The report can
inform you of missing updates or mistakes.

- **Don't file as many claims.** It may be better
  to pay the smaller bills yourself.

- **Be willing to pay more** for your homeowner's
  insurance deductible.

- **Have a good credit report.** More insurers are
  looking at credit reports to determine policy
  rates.

- **Buy your homeowner's, auto, and liability
  policies from the same insurer.** This can
  save you 10 to 15 percent in costs.

- **Make home security improvements.**

- **Check on any available discounts.** Retirees
  or loyal customers may qualify.

- **Look over your policy.** Review it annually
  and see that it is up-to-date.

- **Keep an inventory of your valuables.**[1]

c. Life Insurance

Make sure you have adequate life insurance. The
question, "How much life insurance do I need?"

comes up often. It is advisable to examine these factors: your current income and lifestyle, your children's ages, and sizeable debts you may have. Remember that the purpose of life insurance is to help maintain your loved ones' lifestyles, not necessarily increase them.

If you are considering purchasing life insurance, find out first what the company's rating is. A.M. Best rates the major insurance firms (*www.ambest.com*). You can also find out which companies are more risky by going to *www.weissratings.com*. The company ratings take into account their credibility, financial status, and their claims payment history.

d. Auto Insurance

Automobile insurance protects you from the expenses that occur when your auto is damaged. Even more importantly, it protects you from the costs you may incur when involved in an accident with another automobile. Auto insurance can be expensive, yet you *can* save money by knowing what coverage you need and by shopping wisely. *The Consumer Reports Money Book* explains in more detail the coverage available:

> Not everyone needs the same coverage. The two most important types of coverage are bodily injury liability insurance and property damage liability insurance. Other types of coverage—

medical payments insurance, uninsured motorist protection, collision insurance, comprehensive insurance, rental reimbursement insurance, and towing and labor insurance—may or may not be important to you.[2]

When choosing auto insurance, consider not only premium costs, but also the carrier's claims-paying ability. You can check this information with A.M. Best (*www.ambest.com*).

Customer service is also an important factor. A good auto insurance carrier should have a toll-free number for easy access. The carrier should have employees who are helpful and prompt when assistance is needed.

One way to save on car insurance is to take the highest affordable deductible. Collision coverage is 15–30% less with a $500 deductible than with a $250 deductible. You might also consider whether you need collision insurance on your older car at all.

Other factors that affect your policy costs include:

Your driving record. The fewer accidents you have, the lower you will be able to keep your insurance premiums.

Where you live. High risk and urban areas are generally charged at a higher rate.

How far you commute to work. The further you drive, the costlier your insurance quote.

The type of car you drive. The auto with fewer features or the less-expensive model can help reduce premiums.

Your age. Insurance rates for young drivers can be very expensive. Here are ways to save:

Your child will have lower insurance rates if he/she takes **a driver's education course.**

If your child has **good grades** (B average or better), he/she can get a "good student" discount.

You can insure your child under your name even though he or she uses the car.

A discount is available for college students who attend school more than one hundred miles away from home and do not have the use of a car there.

Refer to Steve and Jill's plan to increase cash flow in Sample 6. They previously completed a *Budget Analysis* (Sample 3) to bring their net income and expenses more into balance. Now they are focusing on key categories where they can make even more reduction in costs in order to increase their cash margin.

When looking for ways to reduce spending, Jill found that she could save twenty dollars more a month in grocery costs. Steve decided he could stay home another Saturday morning rather than go out with his golf buddies. This cuts their costs even more efficiently with a minimum sense of deprivation.

Sample 6

Increased Cash Flow Plan

Name: *Steve and Jill*

Date: _____

Reduce Living Expenses By:	Monthly Reduction	Annual Reduction
Housing	$ 30	$ 360
Groceries/Food	$ 20	$ 240
Clothes	$	$
Utilities/Cable	$ 30	$ 360
Entertainment	$ 40	$ 480
Gifts	$ 10	$ 120
Insurance	$	$
Other	$	$
Total Cash Flow Increase	$ 130	$ 1,560

Start Growing Savings Accounts

Complete the *Increased Cash Flow Plan* (Worksheet Six), taking into account other monthly reductions you can make to generate more cash.

Besides redirecting some of your money towards debt reduction, it is important to consistently set aside funds for expected annual or semi-annual expenses such as car insurance, property taxes, and homeowner's insurance. If you have direct deposit at your bank or credit union, you can have a set amount automatically transferred from your paycheck every month into various savings accounts, including auto repairs and vacations. If you consistently place your tips, bonus checks, and birthday checks into your savings accounts, they will slowly build up.

Once you have a better picture of where you stand financially, decide how to improve your current situation. Have the courage to make constructive changes. For many, this means reducing monthly expenses somewhere. Try to keep your new plan of reducing your expenses and debt repayment for at least three months. The primary goal is to have a positive (as opposed to a negative) cash flow. Once this is accomplished one can move on to long-term goals.

Resolve to take action and do not wait. One can expect hindrances in the future; however, if you are following your overall plan faithfully, those obstacles can be met as they arise.

Bill Consolidation Loans

A consolidation loan may be a temporary solution *if* you change the spending habits that got you into trouble in the first place. It should not be a substitute for discipline. The loan won't be the solution to your financial problems if the root of the problem is not resolved first. If the debt was caused by overspending, that will need to be controlled.

One drawback of the consolidation loan is that people tend to stop worrying about their bills and spend even more money. Many actually make more purchases immediately after consolidating. They mistakenly think that with the financial pressure off them they can be at ease and let up their guard. Nothing could be further from the truth! Another drawback is the consolidation loan's presence on your credit record. This shows potential lenders that you have poor spending habits.

Mortgage Loans

I vividly recall the day my husband and I signed the papers for our first mortgage. We had first calculated the total cost of paying for our first house, including the interest. The total figure seemed ridiculously high. Ever since we owned our first home, we made it a goal to pay ahead on our mortgage. We have saved thousands of dollars in interest payments by paying extra principal on the home mortgage payments.

It is best if families spend no more than 25 percent of their net spendable income on house payments. When they add other monthly home expenses, the total housing costs can easily come to 35–40 percent of one's income.

Plan to Succeed

Developing a manageable financial plan is not enough. We now know it is important to change our old, negative ways of thinking about money. To help develop a debt-free mindset, we must also focus on what words we choose to use. *What we say* not only affects other people, it also has a great effect on us. If we tell others we will never be able to accomplish a goal or that we do not see any way out of our current situation, our words can become self-fulfilling prophecies of doom.

We know that experience can be a great teacher, but the fees for it are high. No doubt we have already met people who learn life's lessons the hard way. Remember: if at first you do not succeed, you should find out why before trying again. As you continue to gain new insights into managing money, you will eventually become money-wise.

Two primary goals of any spending plan are: 1) to reduce high interest debt and, 2) to increase savings account balances. As we stick with these key goals, we will make noticeable progress.

Chapter Seven

Follow Through with Your Plan

"The person who makes a success of living is the one who sees his goal steadily and aims for it unswervingly."
—Cecil B. DeMille

Cecil B. DeMille was a famous movie director and producer. His film *The Greatest Show on Earth* (1951) won the Academy Award for best picture. Among his other films that won praise was *The Ten Commandments* (1956).

DeMille was known for his attention to detail, his perseverance, and for excellence in his endeavors.[1] Very little stopped him when he saw the big picture. When we catch a glimpse of what could be the big picture in our own lives we are on our way to attaining our goals. As we move forward with our financial plans, we can proceed without wavering.

By now you know your monthly spending figures. You have kept a record of every expense you've had for a month. Based on these numbers, you have been able to come up with a personalized and realistic budget to follow. Our focus now is to look at tangible ways that you can follow through with your plan.

Maintain Your Budget Each Month

When you are tempted to drop your plan of action and go back to the old ways of spending and living, stop for a moment. Reflect on how you saw a better way of life for yourself as your financial obligations would be paid off, one at a time.

You may need to make a few minor adjustments along the way. If one change seems too rigid, explore some other options that may work better for you.

W. Edwards Deming was an American businessman and statistician who started the Total Quality Movement (TQM). He studied quality, competition, and productivity in the workplace and was known to be an expert in the area. Deming stated that when we focus on the first 15 percent of a process and get it right, we can be sure that the other 85 percent of the process will continue effortlessly.[2] By following the steps we have covered so far, you have easily crossed the 15 percent mark by now! Keep up with your plan by doing the following:

1. Pay your bills on time.
2. Keep family expenses down.
3. Begin to save.
4. Pay off your credit cards.
5. Avoid and pay off consumer debt.

Pay Your Bills on Time

It seems that some people are more concerned about keeping up with the Joneses than keeping up with their bills. But bills must be paid promptly or they incur penalties. Establish a regular place for bills to be placed so that no matter who gets the mail the bills are all in one location.

It is important to manage your cash flow *and* your time. Husbands and wives need to be accountable to each other when it comes to how money is spent. Communicate with each other about resource allocations. Things bought on "convenient terms" seem to always fall due at inconvenient times. Yet it is essential that bills be paid on time.

Don't think that forgetting about your bills will help. Should you find yourself getting behind on your bill payments, contact your creditors. Do not ignore them or your billing notices. Try to work out a manageable payment plan, and then be sure to follow through with it.

Keep Your Family Expenses Down

It is best to pay cash for consumables. This includes general living expenses, clothing, and entertainment. If you are used to the feel of using plastic for your purchases, switch to a debit card. Enter the purchase amount into your checkbook ledger immediately to aid in cash control. Do not be content with mortgaging your future.

Resist the sales hype. If you shop from a reasonable list, unnecessary purchases won't be made. We are often tempted to buy something because it is on sale and we can save money on it. The other alternative is to not make the purchase and you will save even more money.

A car is a depreciating item and rarely can you get out of it what you put into it. When paying off your car, do not trade it in right away. You can probably drive it a lot longer—while saving for your next car. Keep in mind that a car purchase can be a main source of debt. Without those

121

monthly car payments, there is more cash flow in your budget.

Car payments and insurance expenses add up quickly. If you find that you need to buy a car, try to buy without getting a loan. However, if you do take out a loan, pay it off early. When it comes to car insurance, it is likely that your payments will be less if you have older cars. Also, your auto collision insurance rate can be lower if you have a higher deductible.

After following your budget plan for a month, study what your expenses were. Consider how you can do better next month and other ways that your spending habits can be improved. What is not absolutely necessary can be eliminated. Take another look at how expenses might be cut. Here are some possibilities:

We could save on cable TV costs.

Pet-sitting and plant-watering favors can be exchanged with neighbors or friends when we're out of town.

We could have carry-in dinners more often to cut party costs.

Begin to Save

Remember to pay yourself. Continue regularly to save a portion of your earnings, just as you would pay your monthly bills. If the amount you designate is deposited directly into your savings account, it will be less tempting to spend it. One of your first savings priorities should be to save for an emergency fund.

If you find it difficult to save, think about this: by saving just two dollars a day, after one year those small daily savings add up to $730. Better yet, if you save five dollars a day, you will have saved $1,825 after a year.

Since this is a book on becoming debt-free, I will not delve into the subject of investing, but will offer a word of warning about investment advice. Be prudent when making decisions on investing your hard-earned money. Do not get involved with transactions you do not understand.

There is an old saying: "Save your money, and when you have silver in your hair, you'll have gold in your purse." Whether you own gold in your purse or shares of gold, it is very rewarding to save for present and future needs.

Pay Off Your Credit Cards

One of the best "investments" you can make is to pay off your high interest debt. Pay your credit cards off first. As you pay each one off, celebrate that you are becoming debt-free.

What other money can be freed up so the credit card balances can go down even more quickly? You could have a garage sale and unload unnecessary furniture, appliances, and gadgets. Check your closets for clothing you haven't worn in years and put it in the future yard sale pile.

Avoid and Pay Off Consumer Debt

Pay off loans with the highest interest first. As each loan is paid off, take the amount of money that was going toward the first loan and put it toward your next loan. As you pay down the credit, you will be motivated to keep at it.

Follow through with your plan to pay off loans taken out for expenses like furniture, vacations, and automobiles. Many people have found that the easiest way to lose control of a car is to not make the payments. They also find that a good way to make their present car run better is to have a salesman quote them the price of a new one.

Although school loan amounts may look small, they do add up. Try to finance education with as few school loans as possible. Four years of cumulative school loans may accumulate interest at a rate that leave you owing more money than you'd originally planned.

I read in the *Wall Street Journal* that a growing number of recent college graduates were having difficulty finding work. Rather than continue looking and taking "lesser" jobs, they decided to attend graduate school. So, besides having their undergraduate school loans, they were racking up thousands of dollars in student loans for graduate school. They were putting off the inevitable.

There is no guarantee that it will be easier to pay school loans more easily tomorrow than today. As always, the key to meeting your financial goals is self-discipline and determination. Without self-discipline, the best of plans fail. Habits don't change overnight and it may take months or even years to feel that you have reached the point where you have control of your finances.

When you are tempted to buy more stuff and to charge it, just remember that there are no rental trucks behind hearses. You won't be taking your belongings with you when you go, so buy only what you need now.

The Importance of Health and Life Insurance

1. Health Insurance

   Our health always seems more valuable after we lose it. Today we are dependent upon insurance coverage for good health care, yet health costs are on the increase. The rate of medical inflation is growing faster than general inflation. A costly medical emergency or hospital stay could easily set us back. When signing up for health insurance, you may want to decide on a plan with a higher deductible. You will probably pay less for health insurance coverage each month.

When you receive a bill, review it carefully to make sure you are not being charged unnecessarily. Sign a bill only after thoroughly checking it over. Read your health insurance statements when they arrive in the mail. When purchasing medication, ask for a generic prescription, which could lower prescription costs considerably.

2. Life Insurance

Life insurance is usually the last thing on earth a man wants to buy in life, but it's too late to buy it later. The purpose of life insurance is to benefit those family members who cannot provide for themselves. Ron Blue wrote the following about the need for life insurance:

The basic purpose of insurance is to transfer the risk that one is not willing to take (or is unable to take) to someone (or a company) willing to take the risk in return for compensation. In the case of life insurance the objective is, first, to protect the family income and net worth growth in the event of the death of the breadwinner, and second, to provide protection to maintain the estate in order that it might pass on to heirs, allowing the continuation of capital from one generation to the other. Thus the risk of loss of income or the erosion of the estate through estate taxes is passed on to the insurance company.[3]

As you consider the amount of life insurance you or your family needs, you may want to ask yourself: would your family be provided for at this level? When looking at the amount of life insurance you would like, ask your agent about what the different levels of protection would cost. Your insurance payments differ according to your ideal level of protection, your level of comfort, or your minimal level of provision. It is essential to evaluate carefully the insurance policies you need.

Wills

Everyone should have a will. This prevents the state from making decisions concerning your assets at the time of your death. If you have underage children, you can designate a guardian for them. A will enables you to plan ahead for charitable giving, allowing you to allocate funds to the organizations of your preference. Having a will can also help minimize family disagreements when a loved one passes on. In your will, you can express your preferences as to who will receive your fine jewelry, furnishings, or other treasured items.

Do You Spend and Save Wisely?

	Yes	No	Maybe
1. I can make a pot of coffee at home before I leave for work, rather than get coffee on my way to work.			

2. I can shop for groceries regularly from a list.

3. If I had the choice to mow the lawn myself or pay the lawn guy to do it, I would do it myself.

4. When traveling, I would be willing to rent a less expensive car to save money.

5. I will pay more on my credit card bill than the minimum amount required.

If you answered "yes" or "maybe" to three or more statements, you are on your way to becoming a savvy saver.

Continue With Your Goals

As you follow through with your new budget plan, remember that a key goal is to control cash flow. Another goal is to experience growth in your net worth. As you focus on these goals, you can accomplish your long-term objectives more quickly and easily.

Tips to Control Cash Flow

1. Bank and Credit Union Specialized Services

To manage your finances even better, take full advantage of the *feature services* that many banks and credit unions offer. These can be quite helpful in staying on top of your bills and payments.

a. **Direct Deposit**

Consider having direct deposit through your workplace. You allocate regular and preplanned amounts for deposit directly into your savings, loan account, or checking (or a combination of these).

b. **Automated Bill Payment**

You can pay your bills and loans online. You can arrange to have them paid automatically or all in one sitting. This cuts down on check-writing and postage.

c. **Automated Account Inquiry**

Your bank or credit union can inform you of your balances and recent transactions. This is done through phone-automated voice systems or the Internet.

d. **Protection from Overdrafts**

When you connect your checking account to another account (such as savings or money market), the other account serves as a backup account. This will protect you from overdrawing on your checking account. There may be fees, but this is better than having overdraft charges. Note that there usually is a limit on the number of transfers allowed each month.

2. Keep Yourself in Check

There are ways you can hold yourself financially accountable every day and learn to be a smart consumer. For example, you can:

a. Make it difficult to buy on impulse. Keep your credit cards at home.

b. Use cash or a debit card for purchases. When your debit transaction is processed, the charge amount is electronically deducted from your checking account balance.

c. Make savings systematic. Consider having savings accounts for education, an emergency fund, and property taxes.

d. Deposit bonuses and tax refunds into savings or direct them toward debt repayment.

It is important to monitor your progress monthly. Stay with the goals you have set for yourself. Try different approaches to attaining your goals if you are not getting the expected results within a reasonable amount of time. Be aware of your target dates for accomplishing these goals.

Remember that we need a positive cash flow in order to reach our financial goals. If we find ourselves dipping into savings accounts earmarked for other expenses, it is important to pay back those withdrawals as soon as possible.

Expect Great Results

Benefits and rewards are what motivate you to continue with your plan. You'll look forward to attaining each goal, one at a time. Accomplishing short-term goals can be as exciting as reaching the long-term ones. Paying off your obligations before the target date is rewarding as well. As you do so, you will find that you develop better mastery of your money and, as you see results, you'll become even more committed to your goals.

Chapter Eight

Focusing on Others by Giving

"*Charity is twice blessed—it blesses the one who gives and the one who receives.*"

—E. C. McKenzie

When our main concern is to keep up with our bill payments and to survive financially, it becomes difficult to focus on anything or anyone else but ourselves. Our possessions, or our *felt need* for certain possessions, dictates our actions and our lifestyle.

Some of us have not yet asked ourselves, "How much is enough?" Sooner or later, however, we will need to face that question. Are we satisfied with what we have? Are we learning to be satisfied with our possessions now? Will we *ever* be satisfied with what we have?

Sharing, or Hoarding?

Napoleon Hill wrote, "Riches which are not shared, whether they be material riches or the intangibles, wither and die like the rose on a severed stem."[1] He emphasized that one of the master keys to riches is the willingness to share one's blessings.

As a nation it seems that Americans are getting stingier than ever. Research studies show that the more our personal income goes up, the less we tend to give.[2] But, we *can* learn the difference between hoarding and saving our wealth. When we share our resources with others, we become less attached to our worldly goods. The focus becomes less on ourselves and more on others and their needs.

Generosity is a heartfelt desire to give to and provide for others. This not only includes the giving of our possessions, but also of our time and skills. When we look around and see a generous person, we probably see someone who is genuinely content. He does not give of himself grudgingly; he gives cheerfully.

When I think of the generous people I have come to know and have observed, the first thing I notice is that they are not particularly wealthy people. Yet that does not stop them from sharing what they have with others.

It is easy for us to have a temporal and short-sighted perspective. Yet giving of our resources not only benefits others; it also changes us. Giving helps change our way of thinking about our real necessities. It changes our mindset and our outlook in life. As we become more willing to give of what we have, our perspective changes. Amazingly, our finances seem to work out better when we give.

A generous spirit is a trait we can pass on to our children. We can encourage them to be aware of others' needs at home and elsewhere. A growing number of our children of this generation are accustomed to expect something for nothing. They are becoming *takers* rather than *givers*. Each one of us has the opportunity to set a higher example for the young and to raise the ethical bar by practicing and teaching charitable giving.

I appreciate my parents' example of selfless giving to others. Although they did not have a large income, they believed in setting aside money for offerings to the church. They were generous with others and were willing to share their time and resources with those who needed them. They did not give out of obligation but out of a true desire to help others. Since they were not caught up in a lifestyle of consumption, they were free to focus on the less temporal things in life, increasing the family's satisfaction and happiness.

Our Giving

Our giving can be categorized into three areas: our money, our possessions, and our time and skills. In what areas do we contribute?

Our Money

Julie told a friend she would give more to her church if she didn't have so many bills and loan payments. She indicated that she really did *want* to give, but was unable to. I wonder if it ever occurred to her that she *could* have more control over her bills and her giving. She can do more than just have good intentions. By adjusting her lifestyle choices, she would be able to make this possible.

When we give, it should be out of our love, goodwill, and gratitude. Many choose to give to their local place of worship, where they receive spiritual help. Many also like to give to various charities, some local, others reaching out to different parts of the world.

Our family has been able to help those in need around the world through World Vision, a reputable nonprofit organization. It has been exciting to see how our dollars have helped families in need, with their education, work skills training, and other needs.

We have also sponsored children in Latin and South America through World Vision for many years. It has been encouraging to see our sponsored children's growth and development through pictures, health reports, cards, and letters. Our relationship with these families has provided a means for friendships to develop and grow between people in the United States and other countries. These sponsored children and their families have often expressed their thankfulness for our help and interest in them.

For example, it was a privilege for me to travel to the state of Minas Gerais, Brazil, to visit Rosimeire, one of the children I sponsored. World Vision made arrangements beforehand with Rosimeire's principal at her school. I'll never forget walking into Rosimeire's classroom and seeing the look of surprise on her and her classmates' faces when I was introduced to them. Rosimeire had told her school friends many times that an American family was corresponding with her, but they would not believe her.

One could say that "seeing is believing," because *that* day Rosimeire's friends learned she had been telling the truth all along. It was her special day. Since I was fluent in Portuguese, I spoke to her class in their language, explaining who I was and why I was there. We took pictures of Rosimeire and her friends. Before leaving, I passed out small gift packages that my own two children helped prepare for my trip to Brazil. The school children were pleasantly surprised and grateful.

Rosimeire was given special permission to leave class early and we went to her simple, two-room home. I met her family and some of her neighbor friends. I showed them pictures of my family and we visited together.

I then visited the local World Vision Center, where self-sufficiency skills were fostered. Women at the center were learning sewing and cosmetician skills and how to be business-savvy. This not only improved their personal and business lives; it helped to reduce poverty in the area.

Besides connecting families with children to sponsor, World Vision provides food and health care to orphans and families around the world. It was great to be able to visit with one of my sponsored children. Looking back on that day, I'm not sure who was the happiest, for the pictures show many smiling faces.

By designating part of our income for others, we can help those in our own communities, as well. Tragedy came to our city in Indiana when a fire destroyed a family's home, along with their belongings, and killed a mother and daughter. Our community saw the need and held a fundraiser for the family's funeral expenses. I was pleased when my own daughter took money from her savings account and donated it to this fund for the grieving family. She wanted to share what she had and was able to help the family in a tangible way, which also gave her joy.

Our Possessions

We in America have many possessions, especially by comparison with people living in other countries. Our communities have food banks, homeless shelters, and other local agencies that could use our help.

My mother loved to help others. Her heart's desire as a child was to be a missionary. She had a natural ability for recognizing people's needs and helping them accordingly. At times she opened our home to those who needed a temporary place to stay.

Our Time and Skills

How can we focus more of our time and energy on contributing *versus* consuming? The "entertain me" mentality has permeated our homes, schools, and churches. We spend millions of dollars each year for entertainment.

Rather than thinking about what we can get, maybe we can turn it around and think about what we can *give* of our skills and talents to others. We all have talents that are unique and each of us has been given abilities to do certain things well. Our talent might be teaching, organizing, or helping in other ways.

Karen and other neighborhood moms came together to work out a plan. Their neighbor friend Jane had cancer, and the cancer was no longer in remission. Jane had five young children at home to care for but was growing weaker as her condition was getting worse. So, Karen and her neighbor friends decided to take turns watching her children at their houses so that she could get the rest she so desperately needed. They even made meals for the family, visited Jane in the hospital, and helped out in other ways. Through their actions they showed that they cared and were willing to take time out of their busy schedules for someone in need.

We have seen retired individuals who volunteer their time in schools and develop special friendships with students who need extra help and attention. They visit and help out at nursing homes or take meals to shut-ins. They are involved in community service and quietly contribute to society. These senior citizens have a wealth of skills, experience, and wisdom, which they give to the benefit of many others.

Our Friend Rosa

You may have heard the biblical story of the *widow's two mites*. The rich were proudly putting their grand contributions into the treasury boxes at the synagogue. Then Jesus saw a poor widow give her last two mites. He told his disciples, "This poor widow has put in more than all; for all these out of their abundance have put in offerings for God, but she out of her poverty put in all the livelihood that she had."[3]

Rosa, our Brazilian family friend, was not a widow but a poor, single mother. I recall the day Rosa excitedly appeared at the door of our home. She carefully and proudly unwrapped a plain blanket to show us a frail, almost lifeless baby. I could not tell if the baby was a boy or girl, because this baby was very thin. Rosa informed us that a neighbor had found this baby in a trash can, still hanging on to life.

Rosa took the dying baby, a girl, into her home. She carefully fed, bathed, and clothed her. She gave this helpless child all the love she had. One of the first things Rosa did was buy a frilly, pink dress for this throwaway child.

We saw Rosa with her baby on a regular basis and began noticing how this tiny girl was slowly putting on more weight, looking stronger, and even smiling. Although she had a poor beginning developmentally, she began gaining strength and eventually walked on her own. The good news is that another lady who also had a special love for this beautiful child took her into her home and adopted her.

When Rosa made the decision to keep the abandoned baby, she and her daughter were living in one small room. Rosa had very little income and barely had enough money to support herself and her teenage daughter. But she was happy to make a difference in the life of this baby.

Rosa and her daughter were friends of ours, who lived with us for several months at a time. Just as my mother saw the need to help them, Rosa saw the need to help that helpless baby girl. Rosa did not have many possessions, but she shared what she had. Not only was this abandoned girl blessed by Rosa's actions, but I could see how Rosa's life was also changed for the better. She was so happy to have been able to help.

Reflect on Your Giving

Generosity can lead to a life of happiness and freedom. Remember, the world is comprised of the takers and the givers. The takers may eat better, but the givers sleep better. Let's take the time to reflect on what keeps us from making the contributions in life that we could be making. When we become totally focused on ourselves, our financial situation, and our relationship problems, it becomes more difficult to think of others. We are reminded of the biblical injunction, "Command those who are rich in this present age not to be haughty, nor to trust in uncertain riches, but to trust in the living God, who gives us richly all things to enjoy."[4] May we not forget that our dependence is on God, our Provider, and that sharing with others pleases Him.

Chapter Nine

The Legacy of Debt-Free Living

> "Successful parents raising positive kids need to 'see' their kids as finished, competent, positive adults.
>
> —Zig Ziglar

When our family visited Florida recently we stopped into a new shopping mall we had frequented on previous visits. As we walked farther into the mall, we discovered a large section in the center of it that was marked "off limits." There, to our amazement, was a huge sinkhole (a deep hole in the ground into which surface water flows). The floor in the center of the mall had weakened and fallen through into the hole beneath it. During our earlier visits we had walked on this superficial foundation, while all around us we were distracted by all the shops, the stores, and the "glitter."

I wonder how many of us continue walking through a life where everything appears to be fine on the surface. All it takes is one unexpected event, however, and the bottom can fall out from under us. The financial pressures of life can be powerful. Until we learn to apply wise money principles so that we can have more financial freedom, we will continue to find it hard to cope.

It seems that society has developed a *handout mentality*. This has changed from the attitude of several decades ago that we should first *earn* and *save* our money, then purchase what we need. In our times of prosperity we *can* save, rather than spend. Then, we can use the advantage we gain to retire debts before *we* retire.

We've talked about the *debt cycle* that many Americans fall into. Then, whether we are aware of it or not, our children easily pick up many of our bad financial habits and copy them. Thus, the decisions we make today not only affect our future, but also the future of our children. These decisions affect the quality of education our children will have available, as well as provide a pattern for them to follow.

Desire vs. Discipline

As parents we are responsible to teach our children the wise principles of handling money. If they have been growing up in an indulgent lifestyle, they will most likely be indulgent adults. Today, more Americans than ever have grown up in middle-class homes. This is a privileged generation. Many of today's children are accustomed to the nicer things in life, without having to work hard for them. Some children have not been given the responsibilities of household or yard chores and they have little understanding of the concept of working *at all* for what they need or want.

We don't seem to hear the message anymore that we can become successful by working hard, saving our money, and managing our money wisely. Some children think that if their parents need more money, all they need to do is go to the automatic teller machine. There does not seem to be a correlation in their minds that first we need to earn the money.

Hopefully our children see us exercise financial self-discipline and moderation. We cannot expect our children to handle money well if we do not set appropriate examples for them. It is important for us to discuss the proper handling of finances with them—and brainstorm ways in which we can be wiser in this area. We can use our own mistakes in handling money when teaching our children.

We Can Raise our Children Well

We can teach our children to set realistic goals. Along with that, we can help them plan intermediate steps to achieve these goals. Children can learn to be dependable and punctual by following through on their chores and small jobs. They can learn diligence, perseverance, and how to do their work with care. They can learn to work honestly. It does not matter if their boss or parents are watching them or not. The task should still be done well. Parents who are observant and encouraging can help their children grow to be responsible young men and women.

Children's daily time management skills can transfer to their money management skills. They can learn to budget their money, as well as their time. Parents can use an allowance system so that children learn how to budget what they earn. We can show them how immediate plans for this week and this month can help guide them to reach short-term and long-term goals.

My son has become meticulous about saving money. He began his long-term goal of saving for college when he was thirteen-years-old. He placed a considerable amount of his money into a five-year Certificate of Deposit with a locked-in CD rate of over seven percent. Through this he has learned that interest rates can compound positively for him when he is the owner.

I recall hearing one of Alan Greenspan's speeches in 2002. As Chairman of the Federal Reserve Board, he spoke on how schools need to do a better job teaching basic financial concepts. I thought he had missed a great opportunity to encourage *parents* to teach their children the basics of handling money. After all, parents are their children's primary teachers. We as parents need to accept responsibility for teaching money concepts. We have many teachable moments available to us throughout the year and we must make use of them.

What can we do to help our children become economically productive? How can we help them have a better financial future?

1. We can teach responsibility and discipline from a young age.
2. We can affirm and support them in their endeavors and achievements.
3. We can see to it that they get a good education so they can become independent.
4. We can teach them the importance of earning, saving, and spending wisely.
5. We can emphasize that saving and spending wisely is more important than making lots of money.

Seven Common Denominators of the Wealthy

The authors of the book *The Millionaire Next Door*, Stanley and Denko, wrote about research they had done on those who are wealthy. Interestingly, they found they have seven common denominators, which are:

1. They live well below their means.

2. They allocate their time, energy, and money efficiently in ways conducive to wealth-building.

3. They believe that financial independence is more important than displaying high social status.

4. Their parents did not provide *economic outpatient care.*

5. Their adult children are economically self-sufficient.

6. They are proficient in targeting market opportunities.

7. They chose the right occupation for themselves.[1]

Authors Stanley and Danko researched families who were both "prodigious accumulators of wealth" (PAW) and "underaccumulators of wealth" (UAW). They wrote the following of their studies:

UAWs (Underaccumulators of wealth) tend to produce children who eventually become UAWs themselves. What is expected of children who are exposed to a household environment predicated upon very high consumption, few—*if any*—economic constraints, little planning or budgeting, no discipline, and pandering to every product-related desire?

Like their UAW parents, as adults, these children are often addicted to an undisciplined, high-consumption lifestyle. Further, these children typically will never earn the incomes necessary to support the lifestyle to which they have grown accustomed.[2]

The researchers contrast the UAW's children to the prodigious accumulators of wealth (PAW's) children, who are proving to be more disciplined because they have been raised in a more frugal and economically disciplined lifestyle. Because the PAWs live below their means, their children also learn to become independent and self-disciplined.[3]

Economic Outpatient Care

Authors Stanley and Denko also noted their observations about the adult children who receive "economic outpatient care." This refers to large and consistent gifts of money and "acts of kindness" some parents provide their children and grandchildren. They write this about the adult children:

> They typically lack initiative. More often than not, they are economic underachievers but have a high propensity to spend. That's why they need economic subsidies to maintain the standard of living they enjoyed in their parents' home.

We will say it again:

> The more dollars adult children receive, the fewer dollars they accumulate, while those who are given fewer dollars accumulate more. This is a statistically proven relationship.[4]

I recall the summer I worked for Chuck, a construction company owner. He had a married son who was still dependent on his monetary handouts. Chuck's son would call him often whenever he was in need of money. He believed the answer to his money problems was more money—his dad's money. I wondered how long this pattern would continue. By giving his son monetary help whenever he wanted it, Chuck wasn't teaching him independence.

Chuck could have been more helpful by asking his son to get financial counseling. Better yet, he could have taught him from an early age the importance of: 1) learning to live and get by on limited resources, and 2) understanding the benefits of delayed gratification.

Giving our children an allowance when they are younger can teach them responsibility in handling money. It is better for them to learn the lessons of wise money management with a little money when they are young than when they are adults and have much more money available to mismanage. If we give them whatever they ask for, whenever they ask for it, we can count on their continuing with the same manipulation skills when they are older.

Smart Giving Alternatives

We have friends whose son, Bryan, looked forward to going to Europe with his Boy Scout troop one summer. Although this was a costly trip, his parents could have easily written a check to cover all of the expenses. Yet they decided that *he* should contribute toward the trip. Bryan's parents told him that if he volunteered at the library they would pay him for the hours he worked.

I recall seeing Bryan several times that year as he put in many hours at our local library. He had a part in making his trip to Europe possible and he probably appreciated the trip even more.

Parents can make matches for tangible things, such as college. They can offer to contribute a dollar or two for their child's college fund for every dollar earned by the student. This might decrease the temptation for students to spend more on other nonessential items.

They can offer to buy their children a Certificate of Deposit of $1,000 if they agree to pay their credit card balance every month for a year. That is, *if* they use a credit card. Or, if their child has credit card debt, the son or daughter could be offered a CD of $1,000 if he or she pays off the credit card within an allocated period of time. Grandparents can help financially.

Jane, a divorced mother, believes it is in her children's best interest to attend a private school. Jane's mother also believes in the benefits of a private school education, and the two decide to split the cost of private school tuition. The grandmother is confident in the investment she is making, the arrangement works out well, and everyone benefits. Another way grandparents can help financially is to offer their grandchild several thousand dollars upon their graduation from college. There is an incentive involved, since their grandchildren must complete their college degree in order to receive the money.

Our daughter, a college student, needed a car so that she would be able to participate in an internship. Rather than buy a brand new car for her, we purchased a used but dependable car.

When I was in college, I paid for my private school education. My parents contributed toward small incidentals or gas money when I needed rides home during school breaks. I also had a "pay as you go" motto for my graduate school tuition.

More Money Doesn't Mean Better Finances

Many families with larger incomes have more debt than those who earn less money. If we look at people with moderate incomes who use sound principles of money management, we notice that they are more stable financially.

It takes diligence to get out of debt and stay out and the rewards are worthwhile. Studies show that "financially independent people are happier than those in their same income/age cohort who are not financially secure. Financially independent people seem to be better able to visualize the future benefits of defining their goals."[5] Their focus is on the long-term goals, helping them to process day-to-day choices and decisions.

Our Legacy

A legacy may be anything handed down from an ancestor, such as money, property, or values. Charles Swindoll suggested we appraise how we are doing raising our children based on these four questions:

1. Am I spending sufficient time with the children so that they know I love and accept them and care very much about their future?

2. Am I communicating life goals, a proper value system, a standard of moral purity, a drive for excellence, and commitment to loyalty, integrity, generosity, and honesty to my children? Do they really *know* how I feel about these things?

3. Are they aware that they are worthwhile and valuable? Are they growing up to be positive, confident, secure, highly esteemed young men and women?

4. When they leave the nest, will they be able to stand alone?[6]

We cannot take our responsibilities as parents to train our children in wise money management principles too lightly—or we will pay the cost!

Live with Sound Money Principles

What kind of a legacy are we leaving our children? Is it a legacy of constant money problems or of having our lives in order financially? Is it one of greed and fear of loss, or one of contentment? We may not think so, but we teach our children how to handle money by our actions. Parents who do not live on a budget or spend foolishly find they have difficulty teaching their children sound money principles since *actions speak louder than words*.

Besides teaching our children to follow wise money principles, hopefully we can also leave them a monetary inheritance. Will we be able to leave our home free and clear of debt for them? We as parents can teach our children that the key to wealth, no matter what our income may be, is managing our money wisely.

We have learned that becoming debt-free is more than a goal. It is a way of life and a state of mind. By removing the roadblocks that kept us from reaching our financial goals, we have shown that our spending habits *can be* and *have been* altered. As we continue to save, we will become even more prepared for any unexpected economic twists and turns ahead.

Chapter Ten

Becoming Fiscally Fit

> *"The plans of the diligent lead to profit as surely as haste leads to poverty."*
>
> —Proverbs 21:5

You may have read or heard the parable of the master's three servants. Before leaving on a long trip, the master gave one servant five talents, another two talents, and another one. (A talent is a unit of money). He gave these talents according to the men's abilities. Upon returning, the master met with each of the men to settle their accounts.

As the story goes, the man who had been given five talents had gained five more. The one who had received two talents had gained two more. To these servants, the master said, "Well done, good and faithful servant; you have been faithful over a few things, I make you ruler over many things. Enter into the joy of your lord."[1]

When the third servant showed the master the same talent he had been given, along with making his excuses for having gained no more, the master responded vehemently.

He answered: "You wicked and lazy servant…. You ought to have deposited my money with the bankers, and at my coming I would have received back my own with interest."[2] The master then ordered that the one talent be taken from that servant and given to the first servant, who now had ten talents. His rationalization was this: "For to everyone who has, more will be given, and he will have abundance; but from him who does not have, even what he has will be taken away."[3]

I wonder what our excuse may be for not growing the money we each have been given . . . . . Or, what reason will we have for not living on our income but living beyond our means?

Many people today have been putting the one talent they have into a hole, much like the servant who hid his talent. Fearful, foolish, or lazy, the servant could still retrieve the talent he had buried in the ground, but had gained nothing more.

It is much worse for those who find that the hole they have created is their debt, or credit expenditures. No doubt they have watched much of their hard-earned money disappear into that hole in the form of interest payments. And for some, this hole has become a bottomless pit.

The Pitfalls of Credit

Throughout this book we have focused on the *causes* of our fiscal problems. Erroneous information about credit can also lead to money problems. Some people have the idea that they need many credit cards to build a credit history. This is false. In fact, some financial advisors say it is wise to stick with two credit cards. But even this, if one is not careful, could cause people to overspend if their credit lines are high.

Instead of contacting all three major credit bureaus for your overall rating, you can go to www.myfico.com and purchase a report with scores from all three bureaus. Generally speaking, if you have a credit score of 700 or higher, you are able to borrow at the best rates. An article in *Money* magazine stated you can do the following to help boost your credit score:

Step 1: Be aware of your credit score.

Step 2: Make your payments on time, every time.

Step 3: Don't use all of your available credit. Try to use no more than thirty percent of your available credit.

Step 4: Stop applying for more credit cards.

Step 5: Have at least one card for a longer time period. This would mean two years or more.[4]

Obviously there are many factors that affect one's credit score. Scores can also vary from month to month.

As we continue to refine our budget, we should be aware that many times it is the *variable expenses* that get in the way of keeping our budget balanced. These include what we pay for groceries, restaurant meals, phone bills, entertainment, clothes, and car maintenance. Other variable expenses are health related items, such as medical appointments and prescriptions.

We have all seen how healthcare costs have risen and must realize that a larger percentage of those costs have been passed on to employees. Since last calendar year, our family saw our co-pay requirement for medical appointments double. Many companies have increased employee deductibles and paycheck contributions in order to cover the increasing cost of medical insurance.

The Wall Street Journal reports that, "One in seven American families has problems paying medical bills, forcing tradeoffs between medical, food, and housing expenses."[5] Even those with medical insurance are finding it hard to keep up with medical expenses. The article continues, "The report comes at a time when consumers have taken on high levels of debt, driven by low interest rates, easy credit terms, and increased home ownership."[6] Although lower interest rates have boosted home sales, in general real estate property values have risen. As interest rates continue to rise it will cause hardship for people trying to meet their monthly bill payments.

Not only has the median price of a home risen sharply, but so has the number of homeowners borrowing against their homes. In 2003 the amount of money retrieved through home equity loans and credit lines and through refinancing was $223 billion.[7]

Hans Nordby, a financial strategist, states that:

> Individuals need to ask, "What is my house?" For many people, it's a place where they live and stay until they go out feet first, not an asset for creating future cash flows. It isn't an investment; it's not a source of retirement income; it's a home.[8]

Hopefully those individuals choosing to put their home up for collateral will be able to keep up with their home loans.

Money magazine warned about the risks of accumulating too much debt, stating:

> Any form of equity borrowing represents a lien—if you default, the bank has the right to take your home. While that outcome is uncommon (most homeowners file for bankruptcy or renegotiate payments before foreclosure), these more likely scenarios have consequences almost as dire. You could get squeezed by rising interest rates. You could end up owing more than your house is worth. You could lose your safety net. You could limit your retirement options.[9]

Let's take a closer look at these serious consequences. For those who have taken on *adjustable rate loans* for their mortgages, when interest rates go up, many homeowners will come to find that their finances have become too tight. Ideally, mortgage payments should be limited to around 25 percent of total income.

If these homeowners decide to sell their home and the value of the home has depreciated, they will owe money. Home values have been known to decline locally and regionally, depending upon economic factors. For instance, if the mortgage loan was made for $200,000 and the home was sold for $150,000, the homeowners will still owe more than the mortgage loan amount.

Those individuals who have used up most of their equity line have used up their safety net. If there should be a major medical expense, for instance, you can no longer rely on your home equity to help.

By taking on too much debt, people also limit their retirement possibilities. Credit obligations would force them to make payments to the bank. Instead, why not make payments to yourself for your future retirement?[10]

Selling Our Future to Credit

The *Safe Money Report* states that, "by keeping interest rates so low for so long . . . the natural risk of borrowing from the decision-making process of millions of consumers, investors, businesses, and governments has been removed."[11] This has:

1. Helped sweep aside the last vestiges of healthy restraint in our economy.

2. Opened the floodgates to debt-bingeing by households.

3. Fostered unbridled speculation in the home and home mortgage markets.

4. Encouraged the creation of a massive bubble of automobile credit. [12]

It seems our economy has been running on debt instead of *real cash*. Our economy is like a car, running on gas fumes instead of gas. But gas fumes will only get our car so far. We are still in trouble, and we need the real thing—gas—in order to move forward. Our IOUs and the government's IOUs will only take us so far.

An Uncertain Economic Future

Although it appears that the economy has improved within the past few years, there are indications that the future holds economic uncertainty. One *Safe Money Report* cover story states:

- The largest U.S. budget deficit of all time (is) expected to top $500 billion.

- The most prolonged period of aggressive money-pumping by the Fed in nearly a half-century has occurred.

- The greatest surge in commodity prices since the late 1970s has occurred.

- The sharpest decline in the value of the dollar since 1987 is at hand, and now, (adding urgency to each of these trends) . . . .

- A political situation which could become the greatest single threat to world oil supplies in modern times is here.[13]

We have seen indicators that may well cause us to question what is ahead. Ernest Hemingway wrote, "The first panacea for a mismanaged nation is inflation of the currency. The second is a war. Both bring a temporary prosperity. Both bring a permanent ruin."[14]

Hemingway's opinions had been formed by fighting in Italy during World War I and seeing firsthand the economic changes brought about by World War II.[15] We may not be able to predict with certainty what the economic future will bring. We can, however, prepare as best we can by managing the resources we have well.

Preserve Your Capital

Without a doubt, economic uncertainties are on the horizon. The Federal Reserve has tried to cushion the economy, especially since the year 2000. However, rising interest rates and larger signs of inflation will bring changes. *How can we manage them?* We must focus on preserving our capital, or *protecting our assets.*

Frank and Delores are a retired couple who learned the hard way that we may think we are financially set, yet things are not always as they appear. Around the year 2000, the newly retired couple built a large house with all the amenities and comforts they had always wanted in a home. It was their dream home and it seemed they had done everything right in order to position themselves financially for the future.

Then, due to fluctuations in the stock market, Frank and Delores began to see their retirement savings shrink quickly between the years 2000 and 2002. Their financial advisor warned them that they now had less to fall back on for their living expenses than they had originally planned for.

After much contemplation they decided to sell their large, show home and move to a smaller home that would be more affordable. They had not expected their retirement savings to dwindle as quickly as it did in such a short time span. What had happened?

The retirement projections their financial advisor had assuredly planned for them did not stand the test of time. Frank and Delores did not expect to downsize as soon as they did, but they are content with their decision, knowing they are doing what they can to extend their retirement savings.

With our economic future, which is sure to have twists and turns ahead, we may need to think more of preserving our capital. It would also be smart not to depend too heavily on our projected savings printouts.

Keep More of What You Make

T. Rowe Price Investor magazine tells us why we need to keep a larger percentage of our funds in a money market fund, which offers more liquidity and a more secure investment opportunity. Five reasons to keep part of our assets in a money market fund are to: 1) prepare for emergency expenses by setting aside three to six months of net income in a money market fund, 2) preserve the down payment of a home we plan to purchase, and, 3) protect our college tuition savings. Furthermore, 4) We may need to move some of our assets from our previous employer's 401K to an IRA money market investment, and, 5) as a retiree, it would be wise to have more liquid assets for living expenses.[16]

A way to minimize taxes now and save for the future is to put some of your hard-earned money into 401K accounts. These tax-deferred accounts offer an incentive for saving when you are earning more. These accounts will eventually be subject to regular income tax rates when money is withdrawn. When investing for your later years, it pays to examine different tax angles.

It is important to start now putting money away for retirement. You can sign up for your company's 401K plan, and your employer may even match what you put into your account, up to a certain percentage. If your company does not offer a 401K plan, open an IRA account and start saving.

Earlier in this chapter I wrote how Frank and Delores needed to downsize sooner than they had planned after retiring. They learned that past performance of their blue chip stock investments was not a guarantee of future results.

Blue chip stocks are usually thought of as well-positioned large-cap and mid-cap companies.

No-Load Mutual Fund Companies

If you consider yourself money savvy enough not to need a financial advisor, one option is to invest with no-load mutual fund companies. Financial advisors will be quick to tell you that no-load means "no help." Yet a no-load fund also means you will have more of your money returned to you. This will keep your costs low.

My favorite no-load mutual fund company is Vanguard Group of Valley Forge, Pennsylvania. Its funds are essentially owned by its investors and I like the relatively stable low-cost index funds. For more information on Vanguard Group funds, visit www.vanguard.com or call 1-800-662-7447. Another no-load mutual fund company is T. Rowe Price of Baltimore, Maryland. Go to www.troweprice.com or call 1-800-401-1788 for more information.

Remember: You can get interest to work for you by saving *as much* as you can *as early* as you can. By doing so, you will have the power of time and interest working on your side.

Play It Safe

John Templeton is a mutual funds pioneer who founded the Templeton Funds. When asked recently what he believed to be the best advice for investors today, he emphasized the importance of "playing it safe." Maybe we should heed those candid words coming from someone who has lived many years on Wall Street.

Another veteran investment strategist, Dan Ascani, was asked about what he sees the broader economic picture of the future to be. He stated, "The world is in the first stages of a *massive pendulum swing*—from deflation to inflation, from financial assets to hard assets, from relative calm to out-of-control turbulence."[17] He explained that during the past twenty years the markets have focused on stocks. Ascani continued:

> For at least the next decade or so, stocks and bonds are going to be trapped in a no-man's land of stagflation, chronic deficits, recurring financial crises, scandal, and self-doubt. There will be individual sectors that shine while others go dark. The government realizes there's too much public and private debt. So, it pumps billions of dollars of stimulus into the economy to inflate the currency, to monetize the debt, to pay debts with cheaper dollars.[18]

As we take these warnings and words of advice into consideration, let us continue to do what we can do now to become fiscally fit as individuals and families. Then we will be ready for the future—no matter what it brings.

Chapter Eleven

Believe, Proceed, and Succeed

"All a person would need to make a transformation is an independent mind and an ounce of courage."
—J. Paul Getty

When we are focused more on our relationships, family, education, health, and our relationship with God, the things we own don't seem to matter that much. Ben Franklin wrote, "When you have bought one fine thing, you must buy ten more, that your appearance may be all of a piece; it is easier to suppress the first desire than to satisfy all that follow it." We see that even Ben Franklin was forced to deal with the question, "How much is enough?" in the 1700s.

People have found that a "pay as you go" motto becomes interwoven into the life of contentment. When we learn to manage what we have, save for our priorities, and eliminate debt as much as possible, it can be a very rewarding experience.

Being Authentic

Some of us are not totally honest with ourselves. We deny we have particular habits, or we tend to brush off the *real* causes of our problems. Instead, we could desire to become authentic; we could search inside ourselves and experience authentic lives.

Neil Clark Warren, a respected relational psychologist, believes that being authentic leads to contentment. He wrote, "Authenticity involves one conscious, competent choice after another.

"Every decision is essentially different," says Warren, "but the process is virtually always the same: 1) determine the decision you need to make; 2) identify which data sources bear on this decision; 3) listen to these data sources logging in with their input; 4) evaluate all the data and, using your values and principles, make your choice. Then, 5) follow through with your choice and carefully study the consequences in light of intended goals and desires."[1] When you consciously process every decision, you are making healthy choices.

Dr. Warren also wrote of ten characteristics authentic people have in common. Authentic people, he says:

1. Experience life in the present.
2. Are "free of fear."
3. Offer "positive regard" to others while they're judging issues and problems.
4. Are self-assured and secure.
5. Seek the truth.
6. Have learned to be adaptable to changes.
7. Are grateful people.
8. Enjoy life.

9. Treat themselves and others with respect and dignity.
10. Do not lose sleep over problems.[2]

Authentic people live in the present. Although they may have concerns or questions about the future, that does not keep them from enjoying life in the present. In Thornton Wilder's play, "Our Town," the young wife Emily asks, "Do any human beings ever realize life while they live it?" At times we, also, may ask this question as we attempt to keep up with our day-to-day responsibilities.

We know that worrying does not solve anything, yet some individuals miss out on living life in the present by occupying their minds with worry. Some people worry when they have little money; some worry when they have a lot. It is difficult to be content when worry overwhelms us.

The Quest for Contentment

A quest is a search, a pursuit, an adventurous journey. It keeps us pressing on. In his book, *Finding Contentment*, Dr. Warren wrote that, "contentment is knowing that everything will be all right."[3] This is so even when it might not appear that way or when we may not know what the future holds for us.

We may not be able to control the circumstances around us, but we can do our best within them. Although we do not have control over much of what happens in our lives, we *can* commit to do our best, no matter what happens. Specifying what we may require of ourselves, Dr. Warren added: "This may involve our planning, our imagination, our diligence, our perseverance, and our careful use of resources. If we hitch our contentment to variables like these—the kind we *do* have control over—we stand a good chance of being contented most of the time."[4] If nothing else, having the knowledge that we did our best in certain situations can be reassuring.

Believe and Proceed

Imagine your joy as you pay off all your credit card balances, one at a time. You don't need to wait until *all* of them are paid off to experience that satisfaction. You can experience it one credit card at a time. Picture the day when you write that last check for your car loan or mortgage. Dream of the opening day of that business you have always wanted.

Once you believe you *can* become debt-free, you can proceed confidently with your goals and plans. There is much truth in the statement, "When there's a will there's a way," because we must have the *desire* to achieve in order to get results.

How Close are You to Financial Prosperity?

On a scale of 1–10, with ten being the highest, rate yourself on the following attributes.

Most millionaires attribute their wealth to these five factors listed below.[5]

1. Integrity

2. Discipline

3. Social Skills

4. Supportive Spouse

5. Hard Work

How did you rate?

Debt-Free Is Where I'd Rather Be

Let's look at some personal testimonials from people who have chosen to live debt-free lifestyles.

- My husband is a teacher and I work for a finance company. Several years ago we decided to live on my income and put my husband's salary into savings. Since my husband has his summers off, he buys houses that can use some repairs and gets them ready for renters. Although our income has grown significantly, we have learned to live quite comfortably on one income. We don't drive expensive cars or buy expensive clothes. We enjoy our hobbies and outside activities. We should be set for our retirement.

- My wife and I married when we were young, and we had three children soon after. We bought a modest house I could afford on my income and we lived comfortably on my salary for years. We have never owned a credit card and do not plan on getting one.

  When I told my friends that my wife and I had found a house in Florida, paid for it in cash, and were moving soon, they wondered how we could afford it. The answer is simple. We do not have any debt, and nothing is holding us back. Our friends would also like to retire and move away, but they just don't know how they can, since they are heavily in debt.

The second couple's friends have chosen to let debt control their lives. Which would you rather do:

1. Take a vacation and charge your expenses, or,

2. Save for your vacation and pay cash?

If you pay cash you will likely return with splendid memories and pictures of great times, not to credit card bills. If you develop the mindset of saving for specific goals rather than buying now and paying later, life can be far more satisfying.

Soon after our wedding day, my husband traveled to Texas for a week of business training. We did not have the time or the money to take a honeymoon vacation. We paid our way through college and had little left in our savings accounts.

Since the beginning of our marriage we developed a lifestyle of living on our income and not going into debt for extras. We took our long vacation several years later and truly enjoyed it.

My husband and I celebrated our anniversary at a Caribbean island for a week. Our luxurious hotel room at the resort offered a peaceful view of the lucid, aqua sea, with sounds of the waves in the distance. One day we took a small, private boat to an island where we had a traditional island meal, along with fresh coconut picked from a nearby tree. We spent the day snorkeling, resting on large hammocks, and exploring the island. Another day we took a cruise and enjoyed the music, entertainment, buffet, and magnificent sunset. Still another day, my husband surprised me with a sparkling gold ring as we browsed in a jewelry store. But the best part of our vacation was that it was already paid for. We had saved for it and planned our itinerary, so we enjoyed the trip with no worries.

It all comes down to focusing on what matters most to you in life. Set your goals according to your personal values and you will reach them. It is likely you will strive harder and enjoy it more if you do. Strive for balance, as well, as you consider what is most important to you and your family.

As we proceed unswervingly toward financial freedom, we will succeed in becoming debt-free. As we develop a lifestyle of living on what we have, it will become easier to manage our money. There will be a sense of contentment, and we'll know we make a difference for others. We will be able to direct our focus in life to what matters most to our families and to ourselves. Best of all, we will become money-wise and experience the freedom to live out our dreams!

Afterword

Reading this book may have caused you to think more about what you are truly living for—what you *cling to* in life. Some of us have tried to buy contentment with relationships, homes, cars, shopping sprees, vacations, etc. I'm sure you can add your own ideas as to what has brought temporary *happiness highs* for you, but I'm speaking of a deeper kind of peace.

So often in life we drift along as if we are on a storm-tossed sea. We may have worries, discouragement, and frustration in life, or feel that we can trust no one. But we *can* trust in Someone Who has provided a better way for us. We can trust in Jesus Christ to help us.

Jesus told his doubting disciple, Thomas, "I am the way, the truth, and the life. No one comes to the Father except through Me."[1] We can find deep-down contentment by putting our trust in Him alone.

When we decide to allow Jesus Christ to steer us and we put Him at the helm of our lives, He will be our Captain and will lead us safely to port. We have no guarantee that there will be no strong wind or gales. However, we have God's promise that, "I will never leave you nor forsake you."[2] We can count on Him to be there with us as we make this passage through life, and we can have His unsurpassed peace in it. I hope that you will trust God with your finances—*and with your heart and life.*

Endnotes

Chapter One

1. *Whatever Happened to the American Dream?* Larry Burkett, Chicago, Illinois: Moody Press, 1993, p. 40, 41.
2. "Credit Card Borrowing, Delinquency, and Personal Bankruptcy," *New England Economic Review,* (July, 2000), p. 15–30.
3. Administrative Office of the Courts, Bankruptcyaction.com, 2004.
4. *The Fragile Middle Class: Americans in Debt,* Elizabeth Warren, Harvard Law School, Smith Business Solutions.
5. *The Consumer Reports Money Book,* Janet Bamford, et. al., and the editors of Consumer Reports Books, Yonkers, New York: The Reader's Digest Association, Inc, 1995, p. 138.
6. "What About Divorce Rates?" www.marriage-relationships.com

7. *Debt-Free Living*, Larry Burkett, Chicago, Illinois: Moody Press, 1989, p. 16.
8. www.cardweb.com, 2004.
9. *Investing for the Future*, Larry Burkett, Wheaton, Illinois: Victor Books, 1992, p. 16.
10. U.S. Census Bureau, *Statistical Abstract of the United States: 2001*, 121st edition, Washington, DC, 2001, p. 735.
11. U.S. Census Bureau, *Statistical Abstract of the United States: 2001*, 121st edition, Washington, DC, 2001, p. 727.
12. *The Consumer Reports Money Book*, Janet Bamford, et. al., and the editors of Consumer Reports Books, Yonkers, New York: The Reader's Digest Association, Inc.1995, p. 152.
13. "The Loan Moan," *Homebusiness Journal*, April 2004, p. 52–54.
14. http//twotrees.www.50megs.com/attic/history/04/16.html.
15. *Whatever Happened to the American Dream?* Larry Burkett, Chicago, Illinois: Moody Press, 1993, p. 193.
16. "Dire Warnings Fall on Deaf Ears! Act Now, Before It's Too Late!" *Safe Money Report*, February, 2004, Issue #358.
17. *ibid.*

Chapter Two

Proverbs 22:7, *New American Standard Bible*

1. *Storm Shelter*, Ron Blue, Nashville, Tennessee: Thomas Nelson, Inc., 1994, p. 94.
2. www.nodebtnosweat.com.

3. "Job Shift Creates India Tech Boom," www.USAToday.com
4. *What the Odds Are*, Les Krantz, New York, New York: Harper Collins Publishers, 1992, p. 113.
5. *Master Your Money*, Ron Blue, Nashville, Tennessee: Thomas Nelson, Inc., 1991, 123.
6. *Money: A User's Manual*, Bob Russell, Sisters, Oregon: Questar Publishers, Inc. 1997, 103.
7. Proverbs 23:7, *New King James Bible*

Chapter Three

1. *Money, A User's Manual*, Bob Russell, Sisters, Oregon: Questar Publishers, Inc., 1997, p. 94.
2. "How Much Money Do You Really Need to be Happy?" Jean Chatzky, *USA Weekend*, September 21, 2003.
3. "Young People Cutting Back, Slowing Down in Quest to Find Happiness," Associated Press, January 22, 2004.
4. "Stress: Can We Cope?" *Time*, June 6, 1983.
5. *www.computerworld.com*.

Chapter Four

1. *The Consumer Reports Money Book*, Janet Bamford, et. al., and the editors of Consumer Reports Books, Yonkers, New York: The Reader's Digest Association, Inc., 1995, p. 102,103.
2. *The Millionaire Next Door*, Stanley and Danko, Atlanta: Longstreet Press, 1996, p. 29.

Chapter Five

1. www.greenpath.com.

Chapter Six

1. "Trim Your Insurance Bill," *Money*, June, 2004, p. 97.
2. *The Consumer Reports Money Book*, Janet Bamford, et. al., and the editors of Consumer Reports Books, Yonkers, New York: The Reader's Digest Association, Inc., 1995, p. 263.

Chapter Seven

1. "He Commanded Moses," *The Wall Street Journal*, July 14, 2004, D14.
2. *The One Minute Millionaire*, Hansen and Allen, New York, New York: Harmony Books, 2002, p. ix–x.
3. *Master Your Money*, Ron Blue, Nashville: Thomas Nelson, Inc., 1991, p. 185.

Chapter Eight

1. *The Master Key To Riches*, Napoleon Hill, Greenwich: Fawcett Publications, Inc., 1965, p. 22.
2. *Generous Living*, Ron Blue, Grand Rapids: Zondervan Publishing House, 1997, p. 33.
3. Luke 21:1–4, *New King James Bible*.
4. I Timothy 6:17, *New King James Bible*.

Chapter Nine

1. Stanley and Danko, *The Millionaire Next Door*, Atlanta: Longstreet Press, Inc., 1996, p. 3, 4.
2. Stanley and Danko, p. 89.
3. Stanley and Danko, p. 90.
4. Stanley and Danko, p. 167, 168.
5. Stanley and Danko, p. 46.

6. *Growing Strong in the Seasons of Life*, Charles Swindoll, Portland, Oregon: Multnomah Press, 1983, p. 231, 232.

Chapter Ten

1. Matthew 25:23 NKJV
2. Matthew 25:26-27 NKJV
3. Matthew 25:29 NKJV
4. "Know the Score," *Money*, June, 2004, p. 183.
5. "Medical Expenses Burden Families," *The Wall Street Journal*, June 30, 2004, D2.
6. *ibid.*
7. www.economy.com.
8. "There's No Stock Like Home," *Money*, June, 2004, p. 169.
9. "Risks of Taking on Too Much Debt," *Money*, June, 2004, p. 83.
10. *ibid.*
11. "The Most Dangerous Financial Bubbles of All Time," *Safe Money Report*, April, 2004, Issue #360.
12. *ibid.*
13. "Oil Market Fiasco," *Safe Money Report*, June, 2004, Issue #362.
14. "Inflation Much Worse than the Government Lets On," *Safe Money Report*, May, 2004, Issue #361.
15. "Ernest Hemingway," *The New Encyclopaedia Britannica*, 2002 edition.
16. "Top Five Reasons to Invest in a Money Market Fund," *T. Rowe Price Investor*, June, 2004, p. 4.
17. "The World Economy is a Giant Pendulum" *Safe Money Report*, July, 2002, Issue #363.
18. *ibid.*

Chapter Eleven

1. *Finding Contentment: When Momentary Happiness Just Isn't Enough*, Neil Clark Warren, Nashville, Tennessee: Thomas Nelson, Inc., 1997, p. 77.
2. *ibid.*, p. 132–145.
3. *ibid.*, p. 170.
4. *ibid.*, p. 171, 172.
5. *The Millionaire Mind*, Thomas Stanley, Kansas City, Missouri: Andrews McMeel Publishing, 2000, p. 11.

Afterword

1. John 14:6, *New King James Bible*
2. Hebrews 13:5, *New King James Bible*

Appendix

My Life Goals Worksheet

A. Lifestyle Goals:

_____

_____

_____

B. Education Goals for Self or Children:

_____

_____

_____

C. Family Goals:

_____

_____

_____

D. Career Goals:
_____

_____

_____

E. Vacation Goals:
_____

_____

_____

F. Savings Goals:
_____

_____

_____

G. Investment Goals:
_____

_____

_____

H. Insurance Goals:
_____

_____

_____

Appendix

I. Giving Goals:

_____

_____

_____

Financial Worksheet Forms

Worksheet One

Monthly Expenses Worksheet

Name: _____

Month: _____

Monthly Spending: Page 1

Income	Giving	Home Mtg./ Ins.	Repairs/ Maint./ Furniture	Property Taxes	Water	Sani- tation	Electric	Gas/ Htg.	Cable	Phone/ Cell/ Internet	Groceries/ School Lunches	School Tuition/ Daycare	Misc.	Entermt./ Eating Out	Total

Column Totals   Total - p. 1

Monthly Spending: Page 2

Gas	Car Loans	Car Rprs.	Ins. & Plates	Doctors/ Dentist	Prescrip- tions	Medical Insurance	Assoc. & Clubs	Clothes	Emerg. Fund	Savings/ Invest.	Life Ins.	Vacation	Credit Oblig.	Total Pg. 1	Total Pg. 2

Column Totals   Expenses Total

Total Giving and Taxes

Appendix

Worksheet Two

Monthly Income and Expenses Summary

Name: _____
Date: _____

	His Monthly Income	Her Monthly Income
Income:		
Salary	_____	_____
Annuities or Trusts	_____	_____
Interest and Dividend Income	_____	_____
Pension and Retirement Income	_____	_____
Government Benefits	_____	_____
Rental Income	_____	_____
Social Security Income	_____	_____
Child Support Income	_____	_____
Other Income	_____	_____
Total Gross Income	_____	_____
Combined Gross Income	_____	

	His	Hers
Expenses:		
1. Charitable Giving	_____	_____
2. Taxes		
Federal Income Tax	_____	_____
State Tax	_____	_____
Local Tax	_____	_____
Social Security Tax	_____	_____
Medicare Tax	_____	_____
Total Taxes	_____	_____
Total Giving & Taxes	_____	_____
Net Spendable Income	_____	_____

(Total gross income less giving and taxes)

Combined Spendable Income _____

The Art of Debt-Free Living

Combined Monthly Expenses

3. Housing

Mortgage/Rent _____
Homeowner's Insurance _____
Property Taxes _____
Gas/Heating _____
Electricity _____
Water _____
Sanitation _____
Telephone/Internet _____
Cellular Phone _____
Cable _____
Maintenance/Repairs _____
Furnishings _____
Other _____
Total Housing _____

4. Transportation

Auto Loans _____
Car Insurance _____
License Plates _____
Maintenance/Repairs _____
Gas _____
Parking/Tolls _____
AAA Fees _____
Total Auto _____

5. Food

Groceries _____
School Lunches _____
Total Food _____

6. Insurance

Medical Insurance _____
Dental Insurance _____
Life Insurance _____
Other _____
Total Insurance _____

7. Health Expenses

Doctor _____
Dentist/Orthodontist _____
Prescriptions/Vitamins _____
Optometrist/Glasses _____

Appendix

Health Club   _____
Total Health   _____

8. Entertainment

Eating Out   _____
Movies/Game Rentals   _____
Babysitting   _____
Club Fees/Camp   _____
Vacations   _____
Magazines/Newspapers   _____
Books
Computer Games and
Software   _____
Other   _____
Total Entertainment   _____

9. Clothing/Shoes   _____

10. School Tuition/Daycare   _____

11. Miscellaneous

Toiletries, Laundry   _____
Dry Cleaning   _____
Hair Care and
Grooming Supplies   _____
Stamps, mailings   _____
Gifts/Flowers   _____
Allowances   _____
Pet Care   _____
Other   _____
Total Miscellaneous   _____

12. Debts

Credit Cards   _____
Loans   _____
Other   _____
Total Debts Payments   _____

13. Vacations   _____

14. Savings

Emergency Fund   _____
401K   _____
IRA   _____
College Savings   _____
Other   _____

Other	_____
Other	_____
Other	_____
Total Savings	_____
Total Living Expenses	_____
Cash Flow Margin	_____

(Net spendable income, minus living expenses)

Appendix

Worksheet Three

Budget Analysis

Name: _____

Date: _____

Total Income Per Year: _____

Gross Income per Month: _____

Net Spendable Income per Month: _____

Monthly Expenses	Existing Budget	New Proposed Budget	Action Plan
1. Charitable Giving	$	$	
2. Taxes	$	$	
Net Spendable Income	$	$	
3. Housing	$	$	
4. Transportation	$	$	
5. Food	$	$	
6. Insurance	$	$	
7. Health Expenses	$	$	
8. Entertainment	$	$	
9. Clothing/Shoes	$	$	
10. School Tuition/Daycare	$	$	
11. Miscellaneous	$	$	
12. Debts	$	$	
13. Vacations	$	$	
14. Savings	$	$	
Total Living Expenses	$	$	

Cash Flow Margin = Income/Expenses

$ $

Worksheet Four

Net Worth Worksheet

Name: _____   Date: _____

Assets

Bank/Credit Union

_____	Cash/Checking Accounts	$
_____	Savings Accounts	$
_____	Money Market Funds	$
_____	Certificates of Deposit	$

Investments

_____	Stocks and Bonds	$
_____	Mutual Funds	$
_____	Other	$
_____	Other	$
Life Insurance: Cash Value		$
Company Pensions: Cash Value		$

Real Estate

_____	Home	$
_____	Rentals	$
_____	Other Real Estate	$

Vehicles

_____	Auto #1	$
_____	Auto #2	$
Furniture and Appliances		$
Jewelry		$
Collectibles		$
Other		$
Total Assets		$

Liabilities

Credit Cards	$
Auto Loans	$
Bank Loans	$
Student Loans	$
Equity Loans	$
Personal Loans	$
Mortgage(s)	$
Other	$
Total Liabilities	$
Net Worth	$

(Net Worth = Total Assets/Total Liabilities)

Appendix

Worksheet Five

Debt Repayment Plan

Name: _____

Date: _____

	Balance Owed	Interest Rate (%)	Monthly Payment	Projected Date of Last Payment
Credit card: Visa	$			
Credit card: MasterCard	$			
Credit card: Discover Card	$			
Credit card: Department Store	$			
Credit card	$			
Credit card	$			
Car loans	$			
Bank/Credit Union loans	$			
Student loans	$			
Equity loans	$			
Personal loans	$			
Home mortgage	$			
Other	$			
Other	$			
Total Amount Owed	$			

Worksheet Six

Increased Cash Flow Plan

Name: _____

Date: _____

	Reduce Living Expenses By:	Monthly Reduction	Annual Reduction
Housing		$	$
Groceries/Food		$	$
Clothes		$	$
Utilities/Cable		$	$
Entertainment		$	$
Gifts		$	$
Insurance		$	$
Other		$	$
Total Cash Flow Increase		$	$

Resource Guide and Web Sites

1. Personal Finance Publications:
   Forbes Magazine: www.forbes.com
   Fortune Magazine: www.fortune.com
   Money Magazine: www.money.com

2. Helpful Internet Resources:

   a. CLUE (Comprehensive Loss Underwriting Exchange): www.choicetrust.com
   b. Credit Bureaus

      * Equifax Information Services: www.equifax.com
      * Experian: www.experian.com
      * Trans Union: www.transunion.com

   c. Debtors Anonymous: www.debtorsanonymous.org

d. Fair, Isaac, & Co., credit and credit rating analysts: www.myfico.com
e. GreenPath Debt Solutions (Formerly known as Consumer Credit Counseling Service): www.greenpath.com
f. H&R Block: www.hrblock.com

- This website will help find an office near you and offers a tax preparation checklist.

g. Insurance Company Ratings

- AM Best: www.ambest.com
- Weiss Ratings: www.weissratings.com

h. Insurance Comparison Shopping: www.insweb.com

- Comparison shop for insurance with the most trusted insurance companies.

i. Insurance Information Institute: www.iii.org

- A nonprofit organization that specializes in consumer information for insurance.

j. Internal Revenue Service: www.irs.gov
k. National Association of Insurance Commissioners: www.naic.org

l.   No-Load Mutual Fund Companies

- T. Rowe Price funds:
  www.troweprice.com
- Vanguard Group funds:
  www.vanguard.com

m. Real Estate Portal:
    www.list.realestate.yahoo.com
n.   Research Provider (independent):
    www.economy.com
o.   Tax site (independent):
    www.taxplanet.com
p.   World Vision (nonprofit charity):
    www.worldvision.org